PRAISE FOR ALFRED GIBSON

From "Wilderness Survival Hacks"

This comprehensive guide is a must-have for anyone interested in wilderness survival ... Having thru-hiked the Pacific Crest Trail the insights in this book are a must for those venturing into the outdoors.

— TONY & ALISA DILORENZO

From "Wilderness Lifeline"

This book is a crash course in basic wilderness first aid and beyond. The author discusses some old-school bushcraft tactics that I haven't seen in other guides. My favorite sections were on using plants for medicine and mental toughness for survival.

— POPPY

WILDERNESS MASTERY COMPENDIUM

WILDERNESS MASTERY COMPENDIUM

ESSENTIAL SKILLS AND BUSHCRAFT FIRST AID
FOR ULTIMATE SURVIVAL (2-IN-1 COLLECTION)

WILDERNESS MASTERY ESSENTIALS
BOOK 3

ALFRED GIBSON

Copyright © 2024 by Alfred Gibson

All rights reserved. No part of this book may be reproduced, stored in a retrieval system, or transmitted in any form or by any means, electronic, mechanical, photocopying, recording, or otherwise, without the prior written permission of the publisher, Book Bound Studios.

The information contained in this book is based on the author's personal experiences and research. While every effort has been made to ensure the accuracy of the information presented, the author and publisher cannot be held responsible for any errors or omissions.

This book is intended for general informational purposes only and is not a substitute for professional medical, legal, or financial advice. If you have specific questions about any medical, legal, or financial matters, you should consult with a qualified healthcare professional, attorney, or financial advisor.

Book Bound Studios is not affiliated with any product or vendor mentioned in this book. The views expressed in this book are those of the author and do not necessarily reflect the views of Book Bound Studios.

To the indomitable spirit of adventure that resides in each of us,

May this compendium be your guide through the untamed wilderness, a companion in times of challenge, and a testament to the resilience and ingenuity inherent in the human spirit.

For the explorers, the dreamers, and the guardians of nature's mysteries—may your journeys be safe, your experiences enriching, and your connection to the natural world everlasting.

With respect and admiration,

Alfred Gibson

In every walk with nature, one receives far more than he seeks.

— JOHN MUIR

CONTENTS

WILDERNESS SURVIVAL HACKS

Introduction to Wilderness Survival	3
1. BASIC SURVIVAL NEEDS	15
Finding and Purifying Water	15
Securing Food in the Wild	17
Creating Shelter	19
Maintaining Body Temperature	22
Signaling for Help	25
Chapter Summary	27
2. NAVIGATION TECHNIQUES	29
Using the Sun and Stars	29
Understanding Maps and Compasses	34
Landmarks and Natural Indicators	36
Making and Using a Makeshift Compass	38
Chapter Summary	41
3. FIRECRAFT	43
Basics of Starting a Fire	43
Fire Starting Materials and Tinder	46
Building a Fire for Heat and Cooking	48
Signaling with Fire	50
Extinguishing Fires Safely	52
Chapter Summary	54
4. FORAGING FOR FOOD	57
Identifying Edible Plants	57
Avoiding Poisonous Plants	60
Foraging Techniques	62
Hunting and Trapping Small Game	64

Preparing Wild Food 66
Chapter Summary 69

5. FIRST AID AND HEALTH 71
Handling Bites and Stings 72
Natural Remedies 75
Preventing and Treating Hypothermia and
Heatstroke 77
Mental Health and Coping Mechanisms 79
Chapter Summary 82

6. SURVIVAL GEAR ESSENTIALS 85
The Survival Kit 85
Choosing the Right Tools 88
DIY Survival Gear 90
Maintaining Your Gear 92
Innovative Uses for Common Items 94
Chapter Summary 96

7. WATER CROSSINGS AND TRAVEL 99
Crossing Rivers Safely 99
Building Rafts and Floats 101
Swimming in Open Water 103
Dealing with Marine Hazards 105
Conserving Energy During Travel 107
Chapter Summary 109

8. WEATHER AND ENVIRONMENT 111
Predicting Weather Patterns 111
Surviving in Extreme Conditions 114
Adapting to Different Environments 116
Impact of Climate Change on Survival 118
Chapter Summary 121

9. SURVIVAL PSYCHOLOGY 123
Staying Calm Under Pressure 123
The Will to Survive 126
Decision-Making in Crisis Situations 128

Group Dynamics and Leadership	130
Coping with Isolation and Fear	133
Chapter Summary	135

10. **ADVANCED SURVIVAL TECHNIQUES** — 137
- Improvised Weapons and Tools — 137
- Constructing Long-Term Shelters — 141
- Advanced Navigation Challenges — 142
- Living Off the Land — 145
- Self-Rescue Strategies — 147
- Chapter Summary — 149

The Journey Ahead — 151

WILDERNESS LIFELINE

Introduction to Bushcraft First Aid — 165

1. **BASIC FIRST AID SKILLS** — 177
- Performing CPR in the Wilderness — 177
- Dealing with Bleeding and Wounds — 180
- Managing Sprains and Fractures — 182
- Recognizing and Treating Hypothermia and Heatstroke — 184
- Creating and Using Splints from Natural Materials — 187
- Chapter Summary — 189

2. **NATURAL REMEDIES AND PLANT MEDICINE** — 191
- Identifying Medicinal Plants — 191
- Preparing Poultices and Salves — 194
- Natural Antiseptics in the Wild — 197
- Using Herbs for Pain Relief — 199
- The Role of Nutrition in Healing — 201
- Chapter Summary — 204

3. HANDLING ANIMAL AND INSECT BITES ... 207
   Identifying Dangerous Animals and Insects ... 207
   First Aid for Snake Bites ... 210
   Treating Insect Stings and Bites ... 212
   Preventing and Treating Tick Bites ... 214
   Rabies Prevention and First Response ... 216
   Chapter Summary ... 218

4. WATER SAFETY AND HYDRATION ... 221
   Finding and Purifying Water ... 221
   Recognizing Signs of Dehydration ... 223
   Treating Waterborne Illnesses ... 225
   Safe Swimming Practices ... 227
   Chapter Summary ... 230

5. FOOD SAFETY AND NUTRITION ... 233
   Foraging for Edible Plants ... 233
   Hunting and Fishing for Survival ... 236
   Preventing Foodborne Illnesses ... 238
   Cooking and Preserving Wild Food ... 240
   Chapter Summary ... 242

6. SHELTER AND EXPOSURE PROTECTION ... 245
   Choosing a Safe Shelter Location ... 245
   Building Insulated Shelters ... 247
   Protecting Yourself from the Elements ... 250
   Fire Safety and Warmth ... 252
   Chapter Summary ... 254

7. NAVIGATING MENTAL HEALTH CHALLENGES ... 257
   Coping with Stress and Anxiety ... 257
   The Psychological Impact of Survival Situations ... 260

Building Resilience and Mental Toughness	262
Chapter Summary	264

8. EMERGENCY SIGNALING AND RESCUE — 267
Creating Effective Signals	267
Using Technology for Rescue	269
Navigational Aids and Techniques	272
Interacting with Rescuers	274
Preparing for Evacuation	276
Chapter Summary	279

9. WEATHER AND ENVIRONMENTAL HAZARDS — 281
Understanding Weather Patterns	281
Preparing for Extreme Weather Conditions	284
Avoiding Natural Hazards	286
Surviving in Different Climates	289
Minimizing Environmental Impact	291
Chapter Summary	293

10. ADVANCED FIRST AID TECHNIQUES — 295
Suturing Wounds in the Field	295
Managing Severe Allergic Reactions	298
Field Management of Dental Emergencies	300
Handling Psychological First Aid	303
Evacuation and Long-Term Care Planning	305
Chapter Summary	308
The Journey Ahead	311

Your Feedback Matters	325
About the Author	327

WILDERNESS SURVIVAL HACKS

THE ULTIMATE GUIDE TO CONQUERING THE WILDERNESS WITH EXPERT HACKS AND SKILLS

INTRODUCTION TO WILDERNESS SURVIVAL

A set of tools scattered along the wilderness floor.

The Importance of Being Prepared

Venturing into the wilderness, whether for leisure, adventure or in an unforeseen survival situation,

Introduction to Wilderness Survival

demands a level of preparedness that cannot be overstated. The difference between a memorable adventure and a dangerous ordeal often hinges on the degree of preparation undertaken before setting foot into the great outdoors. The start of this book delves into the critical importance of being prepared, offering insights and strategies to ensure you are well-equipped to face the challenges and unpredictabilities of the wilderness.

Preparation for wilderness survival begins with a mindset that embraces planning, knowledge acquisition, and practical skill development. The first step is understanding that the wilderness does not conform to our expectations but demands respect and caution. It's about recognizing that while the wilderness offers beauty and tranquility, it also presents dangers, from unpredictable weather to potentially hazardous terrain and wildlife encounters.

One of the foundational aspects of being prepared is having a comprehensive understanding of the environment you're entering. This involves researching the area you plan to visit, including its climate, topography, potential hazards, and any recent changes or events that might impact your visit (such as forest fires, floods, or wildlife activity). With this knowledge, you can better plan your trip, including selecting the most appropriate routes, campsites, and times of year to visit.

Equally important is equipping yourself with the

Introduction to Wilderness Survival

necessary gear and supplies. This doesn't mean overburdening yourself with every conceivable gadget but carefully selecting items that are essential for survival and safety. Key items include a reliable means of communication, navigation tools (such as a map and compass or GPS device), a first-aid kit, a multi-purpose tool, fire-starting materials, and adequate food and water supplies. It's also crucial to have appropriate clothing and shelter tailored to the specific conditions you expect to encounter to protect against the elements.

Beyond physical preparations, mental readiness plays a pivotal role in wilderness survival. This encompasses having a positive and resilient mindset and being equipped with essential survival skills. Knowing how to find and purify water, build a shelter, signal for help, navigate without a compass, and identify edible plants can make the difference between life and death. Regularly practicing these skills in a controlled environment can boost your confidence and competence, making you better prepared to face unexpected situations.

Finally, preparation also means having a clear plan and communicating it with others. Inform someone trustworthy about your itinerary, including where you're going, the routes you plan to take, and when you expect to return. This simple step can be lifesaving, ensuring that rescuers have a starting point to begin their search if something goes awry.

In essence, preparing for wilderness survival is about adopting a comprehensive approach combining knowledge, skills, and practical measures. It's about foreseeing potential challenges and equipping yourself to meet them head-on. With the proper preparation, the wilderness can be a source of immense joy and profound experiences rather than a setting for survival struggles. As we move forward, understanding the wilderness's complexity and unpredictability becomes the next crucial step in our journey of preparedness and survival.

Understanding the Wilderness

Going into the wild requires more than just a robust spirit and a backpack full of gear. It demands a deep understanding of the environment you're entering. The wilderness, with its vast landscapes and untamed nature, is both beautiful and unforgiving. To navigate its challenges, one must first appreciate its complexity and learn to read the subtle cues it provides.

The wilderness varies greatly from dense forests and arid deserts to towering mountains and expansive plains. Each ecosystem presents its unique set of challenges and resources. Understanding these environments is crucial for practical survival. For instance, finding water in a

Introduction to Wilderness Survival

desert requires different strategies than in a rainforest. Similarly, the materials available for shelter or fire-making can vastly differ between a snowy tundra and a temperate forest.

Weather plays a significant role in wilderness survival. Conditions can change rapidly, turning a manageable situation into a difficult one. Knowing weather patterns and the ability to read the sky can make the difference between staying dry and warm or suffering from exposure. Preparing for the worst-case scenario, such as unexpected storms or extreme temperatures, is part of understanding the wilderness.

Wildlife is another critical aspect. The wilderness is home to various creatures, each adapted to survive in specific environments. Learning about the local fauna, including which animals are dangerous and which can provide food, is essential. Additionally, understanding animal behavior can prevent unwanted encounters and help source food in survival situations.

Navigation skills are indispensable in the wilderness. Modern technology, like GPS, has made it easier to find our way, but these devices can fail. A deep understanding of traditional navigation methods, such as using a compass and reading topographical maps, ensures that one can always find their way. Moreover, natural navigation techniques, such as using the position of the sun, stars, and even certain plant species, can

Introduction to Wilderness Survival

enhance one's ability to move through the wilderness confidently.

Finally, the psychological aspect of wilderness survival must be balanced. Understanding the wilderness also means understanding oneself. It's about knowing your limits, managing fear, and staying calm in adversity. The wilderness can be isolating, and the mental challenges often outweigh the physical ones. Developing resilience, maintaining a positive attitude, and practicing mindfulness can significantly impact survival outcomes.

Understanding the wilderness is about respecting its power and learning to coexist with nature. It's a comprehensive approach that combines knowledge of the environment, skills in navigation and survival techniques, and psychological preparedness. This foundation prepares one for the challenges of wilderness survival. It enriches the experience, allowing for a deeper connection with the natural world. As we progress, we'll delve into the essential survival skills that build upon this understanding, equipping you with the tools needed to thrive in the wilderness.

Essential Survival Skills Overview

Travelling through the wilderness demands a foundational understanding of essential survival skills. These skills are the bedrock upon which all wilderness

Introduction to Wilderness Survival

survival knowledge is built, equipping you with the tools necessary to navigate, endure, and ultimately thrive in the natural environment. This overview serves as a bridge from grasping the vast and varied aspects of the wilderness to preparing your mind and body for its challenges.

First and foremost, the ability to find and purify water is paramount. Water is life, and understanding how to locate water sources, whether by recognizing terrain features that suggest the presence of water or by collecting dew and rainwater, can make the difference between survival and succumbing to dehydration. Equally important is knowing how to purify water using boiling, chemical treatment, or filtration methods to remove pathogens that can cause illness.

Next, mastering the skill of building a shelter is critical for protection against the elements. A shelter can shield you from the harsh sun, insulate you against cold, and provide a barrier from wind and rain. The type of shelter you build will depend on the resources available in your environment and the specific conditions you are facing. Learning several methods for constructing shelters using natural materials or items from a survival kit can significantly increase your chances of enduring adverse conditions.

Fire-making is another indispensable skill. Fire serves multiple purposes: to keep you warm, cook food,

Introduction to Wilderness Survival

purify water, signal for help, and deter wildlife. Familiarity with various fire-starting techniques, including using a spark, friction, or the sun's rays with a lens, is crucial. Equally important is understanding how to gather and prepare tinder, kindling, and fuel to sustain a fire under different weather conditions.

Foraging for food is a skill that requires knowledge and caution. The wilderness is home to a plethora of edible plants, insects, and animals, but also to many that are toxic. Identifying safe, nutritious food sources and basic trapping and fishing techniques can sustain you over extended periods. This knowledge not only aids in survival but deepens your connection to the natural world.

Lastly, navigation skills are essential to find your way in the wilderness. Familiarity with reading topographic maps, using a compass, and understanding natural navigation cues such as the position of the sun and stars can help you orient yourself and plan your movements. In today's digital age, proficiency with GPS devices is beneficial. Still, it's vital to prepare for scenarios where technology may fail.

As we transition from understanding the wilderness to preparing ourselves mentally and physically, remember that these essential survival skills form the foundation of that preparation. They empower us to survive and thrive in the natural world, fostering a deep respect for its beauty and challenges.

Mental and Physical Preparation

Embarking on a wilderness adventure, whether by choice or circumstance, demands more than just a backpack full of gear and a map. The real journey begins with the mental and physical preparation that sets the foundation for survival. This section delves into the crucial aspects of preparing oneself mentally and physically before stepping into the wild, ensuring you are as ready as can be for whatever nature throws your way.

Mental Preparation: The Bedrock of Survival

The wilderness does not discriminate. It is an impartial teacher that presents challenges and lessons in equal measure. Mental resilience, therefore, becomes your most valuable asset. Start by cultivating a positive mindset. Believe in your ability to overcome challenges and remind yourself that adversity is not a roadblock but a stepping stone to growth. Try to familiarize yourself with common survival scenarios and visualize yourself navigating them successfully. This mental rehearsal boosts confidence and reduces panic in real-life situations.

Introduction to Wilderness Survival

Stress management is another critical aspect of mental preparation. Learn techniques such as deep breathing, meditation, or mindfulness to keep anxiety at bay. The ability to remain calm under pressure can significantly influence your decision-making process and survival chances.

Physical Preparation: Building the Temple

Survival is a physical endeavor as much as it is a mental one. Begin by assessing your physical condition and identify areas for improvement. Cardiovascular endurance, strength, and flexibility are paramount. Incorporate running, swimming, or cycling into your routine to boost stamina. Strength training, focusing on functional movements, prepares your body for the rigors of outdoor activities like climbing, lifting, and carrying. Flexibility exercises, such as yoga or stretching routines, enhance mobility and reduce the risk of injury.

Equally important is familiarizing yourself with the physical demands of specific environments. For example, if you're heading to a mountainous area, include hikes in your training to acclimate your body to the elevation and terrain. For cold environments, practice with the gear you'll be using, such as snowshoes or skis, to ensure comfort and proficiency.

Your body's performance is heavily influenced by

what you consume. Prioritize a balanced diet rich in nutrients to support your physical training. Hydration is equally crucial; learn to manage your water intake and recognize the signs of dehydration. Understanding the basics of wilderness nutrition, such as identifying edible plants or purifying water, can be lifesaving.

Lastly, always appreciate the power of rest and recovery. Adequate sleep and rest days are essential for physical and mental recovery, reducing the risk of burnout and injury. Learn to listen to your body and give it the care it deserves.

As you gear up for your wilderness adventure, remember that the journey begins long before you set foot on the trail. Mental and physical preparation are the cornerstones of survival, equipping you with the resilience, strength, and wisdom to face the challenges ahead. With these foundations in place, you're ready to embark on a journey of discovery, learning, and growth in the great outdoors.

1
BASIC SURVIVAL NEEDS

A tent and campfire in the wilderness.

Finding and Purifying Water

Securing a safe water source is paramount for survival. The human body can only last a few days without water, making it a critical first step in survival. When searching for water, look for natural formations such as valleys and low-lying areas where water naturally collects. Rivers, streams, and lakes are obvious sources, but pay attention to morning dew or rainwater, which can be collected with a clean cloth or container. Be cautious of stagnant water or sources near animal tracks to avoid contamination.

Once you've found a water source, purification is the next crucial step, as natural water can contain harmful pathogens. Boiling is the most effective method to purify water. Bring the water to a rolling boil for at least one minute, longer at higher altitudes, to kill bacteria, viruses, and parasites. If boiling is not an option, chemical purifiers like iodine or chlorine tablets can be used. However, they may leave an aftertaste and are ineffective against all pathogens. Filtering through a clean cloth can remove large particulates before boiling or chemical treatment. Still, on its own, more is needed to ensure safety.

Solar water disinfection (SODIS) can be a viable alternative in situations where none of these methods are available. Fill a clear plastic bottle with water and place it in direct sunlight for at least six hours. The UV rays will help inactivate most pathogens, making drinking water safer. Remember, while these methods can significantly reduce the risk of waterborne diseases, none are foolproof, and caution should always be exercised when drinking water in the wilderness.

Securing Food in the Wild

After ensuring you have access to clean water, the next critical step in wilderness survival is securing food. While the prospect of finding and preparing food in the wild may seem daunting, you can employ several practical strategies to nourish yourself until help arrives or you find your way back to civilization.

First, it's essential to understand the environment you're in, as different ecosystems offer various food sources. Forests, for example, are rich in nuts, berries, and mushrooms, but not all are safe to eat. Identifying a few common, edible plants before your adventure can be lifesaving. Deserts, while seemingly barren, can provide plants like cacti that contain water and nutrients and insects high in protein.

Foraging is often the most accessible means of securing food, but caution is paramount. Always avoid plants with milky sap, a bitter taste, or an almond scent when crushed, as these can be indicators of toxicity. Stick to fruits and vegetables that you recognize, such as dandelions, which are entirely edible, or easily identifiable berries like blackberries. The rule of thumb is: when in doubt, leave it out.

Insects and small animals can also be excellent protein sources. Insects such as crickets, grasshoppers, and ants are widely available and can be eaten raw or cooked. However, avoid brightly colored insects or those that emit a strong odor, as these characteristics can indicate toxicity. Small fish, frogs, and snakes can be caught using simple traps or makeshift fishing gear, but cooking these animals is crucial to kill potential pathogens.

Fishing can be a viable option if you find yourself near a water source. Using a safety pin or a makeshift hook, you can fashion a fishing line from your survival kit's thread or string. Bait can be anything from small insects to pieces of fruit. Patience and stillness are your allies here, as fish are easily startled by sudden movements.

Regardless of your food source, safety should always be your top priority. Ensure all food, especially meat, is cooked thoroughly to avoid foodborne illnesses. If you're unsure about the edibility of a plant or fungus, performing a simple contact test on your skin can help determine its safety. Remember, securing food is about sustenance, not gourmet dining. Focus on calorie-rich foods that will provide you with the energy to survive.

While survival is your primary goal, respecting nature and conserving resources is also essential. Take only what you need and leave the environment as undisturbed as possible. This not only ensures that the ecosystem remains balanced, but it also leaves resources for other survivors who may come after you.

Creating a shelter will be your focus in the next steps of your survival journey. A secure and safe shelter can protect you from the elements and improve your chances of survival. But for now, remember that securing food, while challenging, is entirely feasible with the proper knowledge and a bit of ingenuity.

Creating Shelter

After addressing the crucial aspect of securing food, the following fundamental step is creating shelter. The shelter protects from the elements and psychological comfort that can be vital in survival situations. The art of creating a shelter using the resources available in the wild is both a skill and a craft that can significantly increase your chances of survival.

The first step in creating a shelter is to choose the correct location. Look for a dry spot, elevated and protected from the wind. Avoid areas prone to natural hazards such as flooding, falling rocks, or heavy snow accumulations. Once you've found a suitable location, assess the materials available. The natural environment can provide a wealth of resources, from branches and leaves to snow and mud, depending on the climate and terrain.

A lean-to is one of the simplest yet most effective shelters you can construct. Start by finding a long, sturdy branch to serve as the ridgepole—the backbone of your lean-to. Prop one end of the ridgepole up on a tree or a couple of sturdy branches wedged into the ground. Then, lean smaller branches against the ridgepole at an angle to create a framework. Finally, layer the framework with smaller branches, leaves, and other insulating materials to protect against wind and rain. The lean-to should be built just enough to accommodate you, as a smaller space is more accessible to keep warm.

A simple lean-to shelter.

A snow cave can be a lifesaver if you're in a snowy environment. Begin by finding a drift of deep, stable snow. Using a digging tool or your hands, excavate a tunnel into a small chamber. As cold air sinks, the chamber should be carved out so that the sleeping platform is higher than the entrance. Compact the snow around the chamber to strengthen the structure and smooth the interior walls to prevent dripping. A small ventilation hole at the top is crucial to ensure a supply of fresh air.

Your creativity and resourcefulness are your best allies in environments where materials are scarce. A debris hut, for example, can be constructed with minimal resources. Start by creating a frame with a long central spine and ribs resembling a fish's frame. Cover this framework with whatever debris is available—leaves, grass, and small branches—to create insulation and waterproofing. The entrance should be small to conserve heat and, if possible, create a door with additional debris.

Remember, the primary purpose of your shelter is to protect you from the elements and retain body heat. As such, insulation is critical. Use leaves, grasses, pine needles, or even your spare clothing to insulate the floor of your shelter and keep you off the cold ground. In colder climates, the thickness of your insulation can make the difference between a cold, sleepless night and restful warmth.

Creating a shelter in the wilderness is more than survival; it's about using the environment to your advantage, respecting nature's resources, and ensuring your safety until you can reach help or make it out on your own. With practice and knowledge, the ability to create a shelter can empower you to face the challenges of the wild with confidence.

Maintaining Body Temperature

In the wilderness, your ability to maintain an optimal body temperature can mean the difference between a challenging adventure and a life-threatening ordeal. The human body operates within a narrow temperature range, and when exposed to the extremes of the wilderness, maintaining this balance becomes a critical survival skill.

First and foremost, understanding the basics of how your body loses heat is essential. There are four primary ways:

- **Conduction** (transfer of heat through direct contact with objects).
- **Convection** (losing heat to the surrounding air cooler than your body).
- **Evaporation** (loss of heat as sweat evaporates from your skin).
- **Radiation** (emission of heat from your body to your surroundings).

Knowing these principles, you can employ several hacks to maintain your body temperature effectively.

Layering your clothing is a fundamental strategy. It's not just about piling on as many clothes as possible but about understanding the function of each layer:

- A moisture-wicking base layer to keep your skin dry.
- An insulating layer to trap body heat.
- A waterproof and windproof outer layer to protect against the elements.

This system allows you to adjust your insulation according to activity level and the weather, preventing overheating and hypothermia.

In cold conditions, your head and extremities are particularly vulnerable to heat loss. Wearing a hat or a balaclava can significantly reduce heat escape from your head. At the same time, gloves and woolen socks protect your hands and feet. Consider stuffing your jacket or pants with dry leaves, grass, or newspaper in extreme cold for additional insulation. This might seem unconventional, but such improvisation can be lifesaving in a survival situation.

Staying dry is another crucial aspect of maintaining body temperature. Wet clothing loses its insulating properties and can lead to rapid heat loss through conduction. If you fall into the water or your clothes get wet from rain or sweat, prioritize finding shelter and changing into dry clothes if available. When you can't change, try to wring out your clothes as much as possible and use your body heat to dry them.

At night, the challenge of staying warm intensifies as temperatures drop. If you've managed to create a shelter, the next step is to build a bed that insulates you from the ground. A simple bed can be made from branches, leaves, or pine needles. The goal is to create a barrier that minimizes heat loss to the ground through conduction. Additionally, using a fire for warmth is a classic survival technique. However, ensuring your shelter is well-ventilated is crucial to avoid carbon monoxide poisoning.

Lastly, remember that your body needs fuel to generate heat. Consuming high-energy foods and staying hydrated helps your body maintain its core temperature. Even simple actions like sipping warm water or hot tea can boost a significant warmth from the inside out.

As we transition from the necessity of creating a shelter to the importance of signaling for help, remember that maintaining your body temperature is not just about comfort but survival. The strategies outlined here are designed to keep you alive and functional, enabling you to take the following steps toward rescue and safety.

Signaling for Help

Having discussed the importance of maintaining body temperature in a survival situation, it's equally vital to understand how to signal for help effectively. Being stranded in the wilderness is daunting, but knowing how to attract the attention of rescuers can significantly increase your chances of survival. This section delves into practical and innovative ways to signal for help when lost or distressed.

Ensuring visibility is the first principle in signaling for help. Bright colors stand out against the natural backdrop, so if you have any brightly colored clothing or materials, use them to your advantage. Lay them out in an open area or tie them to a high point to catch the eye of passing rescuers.

Smoking is one of the most traditional yet effective methods to signal for help. A fire serves multiple survival purposes, but with the proper technique, it can also be a powerful signal. Add green vegetation, rubber, or oil to your fire to create visible smoke during the day. This produces thick, white smoke that can be seen for miles. A bright fire is visible from a great distance at night, so focus on maintaining an intense blaze.

Reflective objects can be lifesavers in signaling for help. When it catches the sun, the flash of a mirror can be seen from far away, even by aircraft. If you don't have a mirror, any reflective surface, such as a piece of aluminum foil, a CD, or even the shiny side of a survival blanket, can work. Practice aiming the reflection toward your intended target for maximum effect.

Sound can be your best ally when visibility is low, or you're in dense foliage. Three loud, evenly spaced noises (blows on a whistle, gunshots, or even banging rocks together) are universally recognized as a distress signal. Repeat this signal at regular intervals to help rescuers locate you.

In open spaces, creating prominent symbols on the ground can attract the attention of search planes. Use rocks, logs, or even make trenches in the soil to spell out "SOS" or "HELP." Make sure these symbols are as large and contrasted against the environment to be visible from the air.

Finally, while it might seem counterintuitive, staying in one place increases your chances of being found. A moving target is more challenging to locate. Hence, you need to be sure of your direction to create a base where you can signal for help, maintain your basic needs, and wait for rescue.

Incorporating these signaling techniques into your survival strategy can dramatically increase your visibility and the likelihood of being rescued. Remember, the goal is to make it as easy as possible for rescuers to find you, so use these methods wisely and persistently.

Chapter Summary

- Understanding your environment is crucial for finding food in the wilderness, with different ecosystems offering varied resources like nuts, berries, game, and fish.
- Foraging for plant-based foods requires knowledge to distinguish between edible and toxic plants, focusing on universally edible plants like dandelions and cattails.
- Hunting and trapping can provide protein through small game or larger animals if one has the necessary skills and patience.
- Fishing, using improvised gear like a branch for a pole or creating simple traps, offers a safer alternative for food, as fish are less likely to carry diseases affecting humans.
- Safety is paramount when securing food in the wild, including cooking food thoroughly and avoiding consumption of unidentified plants or animals.
- Conservation and respect for nature are emphasized, taking only what is needed and minimizing environmental impact to preserve resources for future generations.

- Shelter creation is a crucial survival skill, with different techniques suited to various environments, from lean-tos in forests to snow caves in snowy conditions.
- Maintaining body temperature through strategies like layering clothing, staying dry, and building insulated shelters is critical, as is signaling for help using visual and auditory signals to increase chances of rescue.

2
NAVIGATION TECHNIQUES

| An explorer using a compass and map at night.

Using the Sun and Stars

In the vast and unpredictable wilderness, the sun and stars are not just celestial bodies that light up the sky;

they are ancient navigational tools that have guided explorers and adventurers through the ages. Understanding how to use these natural phenomena for navigation can be a lifesaver when modern technology fails or is unavailable. This section delves into practical techniques for using the sun and stars to find your way in the wilderness.

Navigating by the Sun

The sun rises in the east and sets in the west - a fundamental principle that can help orient you in the wilderness. During the day, the sun's position can give you a general sense of direction. The Shadow-Tip Method is a straightforward method to find your direction, which involves using a stick and the sun to find the north.

1. Place a stick vertically into the ground to cast a shadow.
2. Mark the tip of the shadow with a stone or any small object. This marks the west direction.
3. Wait about 15 minutes, and you'll notice the shadow moves.
4. Mark the new position of the shadow tip. This marks the east direction.

5. Draw a line between the two marks to get an east-west line. Standing with the first mark (west) to your left and the second mark (east) to your right, you are now facing north.

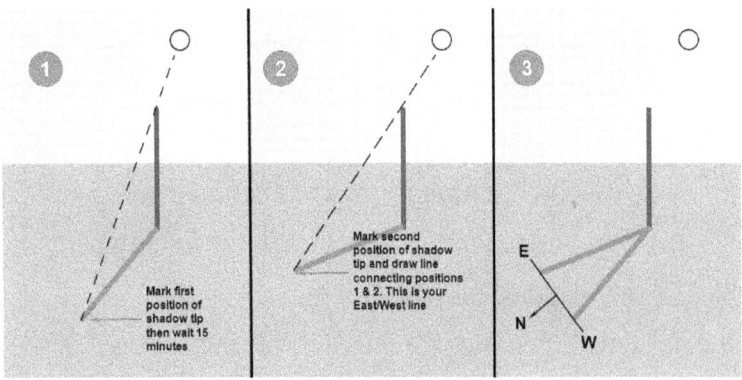

The Shadow-Tip Method by @AlamoAreaBSA.

This method is most effective around noon when the sun is at its highest point in the sky. It's a quick way to establish cardinal directions. It can be instrumental in open areas where the sun is visible.

Navigating by the Stars

At night, the stars take over as guides. Polaris, also known as the North Star, is the most well-known navigation star. It's almost directly above the North Pole, making it a reliable north indicator in the Northern Hemisphere.

To find Polaris:

1. Locate the Big Dipper, a prominent group of seven stars that resembles a ladle or spoon.
2. Look at the "edge" of the Big Dipper opposite the handle to find the two stars forming the bowl's outer part. These are the "pointer" stars.
3. Draw an imaginary line connecting these two stars and extend it outward, about five times the distance between them.
4. This line points directly to Polaris, the last star in the handle of the Little Dipper.

Polaris in the night sky by Science Sparks.

The Southern Cross (Crux) is a crucial constellation for finding south in the Southern Hemisphere. Extending an imaginary line from the top to the bottom of the Southern Cross and projecting it towards the horizon can approximate the south direction.

The Southern Cross by The Nine Planets.

Practical Tips

- Practice these methods before you need them. Familiarity with the sun's path and the night sky will make navigation much easier when the situation arises.
- Remember that environmental factors like mountains, valleys, and dense forests can affect your perception of the sun's position and the visibility of stars. Always cross-check with other navigation methods if possible.

- Remember the seasonal variations in the sun's path and the visibility of constellations. The more you understand these patterns, the more accurately you can navigate.

By mastering these ancient techniques of using the sun and stars for navigation, you equip yourself with valuable skills that enhance your wilderness survival toolkit. While modern navigation tools are convenient and precise, the reliability and universality of celestial navigation make it an indispensable backup method for any adventurer.

Understanding Maps and Compasses

Mastering the art of navigation is akin to holding the key to your safety and direction. While the celestial bodies offer a natural compass, the tools of the modern explorer —maps and compasses—provide precision and reliability that can be lifesaving in unfamiliar terrains. This section delves into the foundational skills of understanding and utilizing these indispensable tools.

Maps are not merely pieces of paper adorned with lines and symbols; they are comprehensive guides to the landscape, detailing topography, water sources, trails, and other critical landmarks. To effectively use a map, one must first become familiar with its scale, which indicates the relationship between distances on the map and the actual distances on the ground. Understanding scale is crucial for estimating travel times and distances. Learning to interpret the various symbols and colors is essential for identifying natural features, artificial structures, and other critical navigational aids.

Complementing the map, the compass serves as the navigator's steadfast ally, offering direction when landmarks are invisible or when darkness veils the path. The essential skill of aligning the compass needle with the magnetic north allows travelers to establish their bearing—a fundamental step in navigating from one point to another. However, the true art of compass use involves more nuanced skills, such as "taking a bearing," which enables one to determine the direction of a specific landmark or feature on the map. This technique involves aligning the compass with the desired destination on the map and then translating that direction into the physical environment.

The synergy between map and compass is where the magic of navigation unfolds. By placing the compass on the map and aligning it with the map's orientation and the landscape, adventurers can chart a course through the wilderness, making adjustments as necessary based on the terrain and other factors. This method, known as "triangulation," can also help pinpoint one's current location using visible landmarks and their corresponding map representations.

While technology offers modern tools such as GPS devices, the fundamental skills of map and compass navigation remain invaluable. Electronic devices can fail due to battery depletion, damage, or signal loss, making traditional navigation skills an essential backup. Moreover, manually charting a course and connecting with the landscape fosters a deeper understanding and appreciation of the natural world.

As we transition from the celestial guidance of the sun and stars to the earthbound cues of landmarks and natural indicators, the importance of a well-rounded navigational skill set becomes clear. The ability to read the land and sky, interpret maps, and utilize a compass forms a comprehensive toolkit that empowers the wilderness explorer to venture confidently into the unknown, secure in the knowledge that they possess the skills to find their way.

Landmarks and Natural Indicators

In the wilderness, where modern navigation tools might not always be available, understanding how to use landmarks and natural indicators can be a lifesaver. This section delves into the art of navigating by observing the natural environment. This skill has guided explorers and indigenous peoples long before the invention of the compass and GPS.

Landmarks are distinctive features in the landscape that can help you orient yourself and navigate from one place to another. These can be anything from a uniquely shaped tree, a large rock formation, a mountain peak, or even an artificial structure like a tower or building visible from a distance. The key to effectively using landmarks is to choose unmistakable and visible features from afar. When you identify a landmark, it's crucial to note its direction about your current position. Keep the landmark in sight as you move to maintain your sense of direction.

However, the wilderness often requires more than just landmark navigation, especially in dense forests or areas with scarce distinctive features. This is where natural indicators come into play. Nature provides its navigation tools if you know where to look.

The Sun: The most apparent natural indicator is the sun. Rising in the east and setting in the west, the sun can provide a general sense of direction. In the northern hemisphere, the sun will be due south in the middle of the day, while in the southern hemisphere, it will be due north.

The Moon and Stars: At night, the moon and stars serve as celestial guides. The North Star (Polaris) remains fixed in the northern sky and directly aligns with the Earth's rotational axis. Finding Polaris can help you determine the north direction. If the moon rises before sunset, its illuminated side will face west; if it rises after midnight, its illuminated side will face east.

Vegetation: Plants can also indicate direction. In the northern hemisphere, moss tends to grow on the northern side of trees because it prefers shaded, moist environments. Similarly, trees with thicker branches on one side often indicate the direction of the prevailing wind, which can be another clue to orientation.

Water Flow: In many landscapes, rivers and streams flow in a consistent direction, often towards more significant bodies of water. By understanding the local geography, you can use the direction of water flow to guide your path.

Mastering landmarks and natural indicators for navigation requires practice and attentiveness to the environment. By developing these skills, you can enhance your ability to move through the wilderness confidently, even when modern navigation tools are not an option. As we progress, we'll explore how to refine your navigation skills by making and using makeshift tools, ensuring you're never truly lost in the wild.

Making and Using a Makeshift Compass

In the heart of the wilderness, where the modern conveniences of GPS and digital compasses are beyond reach, the savvy survivor must return to the roots of ancient navigation. One ingenious and surprisingly simple method involves creating a makeshift compass. This technique can be a game-changer for those disoriented among nature's vast expanses.

To begin, you'll need to find a small, flat surface that can float on water—a leaf, a piece of bark, or even a paper scrap if you have one. Next, locate a needle or a thin, straight piece of metal. A small, straight twig can serve as a rudimentary substitute in a pinch, though it's less than ideal.

The magic ingredient in this survival hack is magnetism. By magnetizing the needle, you give it the properties needed to align with the Earth's magnetic field, turning it into a compass needle. To magnetize your needle, you can use silk or wool fabric. If you're wearing a cotton shirt, the friction from vigorously rubbing the needle across your clothing might also do the trick, albeit less effectively. Running the needle through your hair several times can also magnetize it without fabric, thanks to the static electricity generated.

Once magnetized, place your needle gently on the flat surface you've prepared. This makeshift raft then needs to be set afloat on still water. A small puddle, a calm pond, or even a cupped hand filled with water can serve as your navigational arena. The key is to ensure that the water is as motionless as possible to prevent artificial movement of the needle.

As the needle settles, it will slowly orient itself along the north-south axis, with one end pointing towards the magnetic north. It's important to note that this method indicates magnetic north, which can vary slightly from true north depending on your global location. However, in a survival situation, this distinction is often a minor concern compared to the immediate need to establish a general direction.

You can now start making informed decisions about your movement using your makeshift compass. By knowing north, you can deduce the other cardinal directions—east, west, and south—and choose your path accordingly. While not as precise as modern navigational tools, this method can provide a crucial advantage in finding your way to safety or reaching a destination when other means are unavailable.

Remember, the effectiveness of a makeshift compass can be influenced by nearby magnetic fields generated by large metal objects, so it's wise to use this method in a clear area away from potential interference. With practice, creating and using a makeshift compass can become a valuable skill in your wilderness survival toolkit, bridging the gap between ancient wisdom and modern survival techniques.

Chapter Summary

- The sun and stars have been used for navigation in the wilderness for ages, offering a reliable method when modern technology is unavailable.
- The Shadow-Tip Method utilizes a stick and the sun to find north by marking the shadow's movement, effective around noon.
- Polaris (the North Star) indicates north in the Northern Hemisphere at night, found by extending a line from the Big Dipper's pointer stars.
- In the Southern Hemisphere, the Southern Cross constellation helps find south by extending a line from its top to bottom toward the horizon.
- Maps and compasses provide precision in navigation, with skills in reading map scales and symbols and using a compass to find bearings essential.
- Landmarks and natural indicators like the sun's position, moon phases, star positions, and vegetation growth offer guidance without tools.

- A makeshift compass can be created with a magnetized needle and a floating surface in water, pointing towards magnetic north.
- Natural navigation techniques include observing the sun's movement, moon phases, stars like Polaris, and following rivers or streams, requiring practice and attention to detail.

3

FIRECRAFT

A campfire in the wilderness surrounded by five campers.

Basics of Starting a Fire

Mastering the art of firecraft begins with understanding the basics of starting a fire. This skill is a cornerstone of wilderness survival and a gateway to warmth, safety, and comfort in the great outdoors. Igniting a flame in the wilderness might seem daunting at first. Still, it becomes an achievable task with the proper knowledge and techniques.

The first step in starting a fire is selecting an appropriate site. Look for a location sheltered from the wind yet well-ventilated to ensure the smoke doesn't become a nuisance. It's crucial to clear the area of any debris, dry leaves, or anything that could catch fire unintentionally. Creating a small pit or ring of rocks can help contain the fire and reduce its impact on the surrounding environment.

Once the site is prepared, the next step is gathering materials. Fire needs three elements to thrive: **heat**, **fuel**, and **oxygen**. These elements form the "fire triangle," a concept essential for successful fire starting. The initial focus should be collecting tinder, which consists of small, easily ignitable materials that catch fire with minimal heat. Examples include dry leaves, grass, pine needles, or even lint from your pockets.

Following tinder, kindling is the next type of material to gather. Kindling consists of small sticks and twigs that can catch fire from the burning tinder. Kindling aims to build a small, steady flame to ignite larger wood pieces. Choosing kindling that's dry and snaps easily is essential, as moisture can hinder its ability to burn.

The final step in the preparation phase is collecting fuel wood. These larger pieces of wood will keep the fire burning for an extended period. When selecting fuel wood, aim for dry pieces roughly the size of your wrist or larger. Avoid using green or freshly cut wood, as it contains moisture that makes it difficult to burn.

With all the materials gathered, it's time to assemble the fire. A popular method is the teepee structure, where kindling is arranged in a cone shape around the tinder. This setup allows air to circulate freely, feeding oxygen to the flames. Once the structure is in place, the next step is to ignite the tinder. This can be done using matches, a lighter, or even a fire starter if you're practicing primitive firecraft techniques.

As the tinder catches fire, gently blow on the base of the flame to provide additional oxygen, which will help the fire grow. Once the kindling begins to burn, gradually add larger pieces of fuel wood, careful not to smother the flames. The fire will become self-sufficient with patience and careful attention, providing warmth, light, and a means to cook food.

Starting a fire in the wilderness is a skill that embodies the essence of survival and self-reliance. By understanding the basics of firecraft, you're not only preparing yourself for the challenges of the wild but also connecting with an ancient practice that has been essential to human survival for millennia.

Fire Starting Materials and Tinder

After understanding the basics of starting a fire, it's crucial to delve deeper into the materials that can transform a spark into a blaze: fire-starting materials and tinder. This section aims to equip you with the knowledge to identify and utilize various natural and man-made materials that can be your best allies in igniting a fire under challenging conditions.

Tinder is the foundation of building a fire. It consists of any material that catches fire easily and burns quickly. The right tinder can distinguish between warmth and hypothermia, light and darkness in the wilderness. Natural tinders are abundant in the wild; you must know where to look. Dry leaves, grass, and pine needles can serve as excellent tinder, provided they are completely dry. Birch bark, with its natural oils, can catch fire even when damp. Another invaluable resource is deadwood, specifically the tiny twigs and branches that snap off easily, indicating their dryness.

Carrying your tinder can be a game-changer for those who like to come prepared. Cotton balls soaked in petroleum jelly, dryer lint, or even finely shredded paper can be compact, lightweight additions to your survival kit. These materials catch fire quickly and sustain a flame long enough to ignite larger pieces of kindling.

Moving beyond tinder, kindling is the next step in

building your fire. Kindling consists of slightly larger materials than tinder, such as small sticks and branches, which will burn longer and hotter, allowing you to add larger pieces of wood to build your fire. The key with kindling, as with tinder, is ensuring it's dry. Look for dead branches on trees or the forest floor that have not been exposed to moisture.

Creativity in finding fire-starting materials can save the day in environments where natural materials are scarce or wet. Certain fungi, like the tinder fungus found on the side of trees, can be used as tinder. Paper, cardboard, or plastic chips can be used as emergency tinder in urban or coastal survival scenarios. However, it's essential to be mindful of the environmental impact.

The process of gathering tinder and kindling is as much about preparation as it is about observation. Developing an eye for spotting potential fire-starting materials as you move through different environments is a skill that improves with practice. Always collect more tinder and kindling than you think you'll need; it's better to have it and not need it than the other way around.

As we transition from the essentials of fire-starting materials and tinder, the next step in our firecraft journey involves building a fire that burns and serves specific purposes, such as heat and cooking. It is crucial to understand the properties of different materials and how they contribute to your fire-making efforts. With the proper preparation and knowledge, creating fire can transform a survival situation, providing warmth, light, and a means to cook food and purify water.

Building a Fire for Heat and Cooking

Having equipped ourselves with the knowledge of gathering suitable materials and tinder, let's delve into the art of building a fire that not only warms but also serves as a reliable cookstove in the wilderness. This skill is fundamental to survival and comfort in the outdoors, transforming a daunting night into a manageable, even cozy, experience.

First and foremost, select a safe location for your fire. It should avoid overhanging branches, dry grass, and other flammable materials. A bare dirt patch is ideal. If the ground is wet or covered in snow, you can create a platform using green logs or stones to insulate your fire from the dampness. Remember, safety is paramount; always consider the direction of the wind to prevent the fire from spreading.

Once you've chosen your spot, it's time to lay the foundation. If you're aiming for heat, a teepee or cone structure is highly effective. Start by placing your tinder bundle in the center, then lean small twigs and kindling around it, forming a cone. This structure allows air to circulate freely, feeding oxygen to the flames and encouraging a robust and steady burn.

For cooking, adaptability is critical. A fire lay that offers stability and adjustable heat is the log cabin build. After igniting your tinder, stack larger sticks around the flames in a square, log cabin style. This method supports your cooking vessel and creates a bed of hot coals that provide consistent, controllable heat.

Lighting the fire is a moment of truth. Ignite your tinder, gently at first, to catch the smaller kindling. As the fire grows, feed it progressively larger pieces of wood, always mindful not to smother the flames. Patience is crucial; a fire rushed is a fire extinguished.

Managing your fire for cooking involves a delicate balance. Initially, you'll want high flames to boil water or cook foods quickly. As the fire matures, it will produce coals. These embers are your best tool for simmering or slow-cooking, offering even heat without the risk of burning your meal. Moving coals closer or further from your pot can adjust the temperature, giving you control over your cooking environment.

Remember, a fire is a living entity in the wilderness. It requires attention and respect to maintain. Keep a supply of wood readily available to feed it as needed, but also be ready to let it die down when it's time to rest. Before retiring or leaving your camp, ensure the fire is completely extinguished. Douse it with water, stir the ashes, and check for warmth. A fire left unattended can quickly become a disaster.

In the next steps of our journey through firecraft, we'll explore how this essential survival tool can also be a beacon of hope and rescue. When done correctly, signaling with fire can guide rescuers to your location, turning a difficult situation into a story of survival and resilience.

Signaling with Fire

The ability to signal for help can mean the difference between life and death. While there are many methods to signal for rescue, using fire is one of the most effective, especially in vast, uninhabited areas. Whilst we've already briefly discussed "Signaling for Help" in Chapter 1, this section delves into the art of signaling with fire, providing practical advice to enhance your chances of being spotted by rescuers.

Firstly, it's crucial to understand the basics of creating a signal fire. Unlike a fire for warmth or cooking, a signal fire must be visible from a great distance. To achieve this, location is vital. Ideally, your signal fire should be positioned on high ground or in a clearing unobstructed by trees or other terrain features. Visibility from the air and the ground should be your primary consideration.

Once you've selected a suitable location, the next step is to prepare the fire. You'll want to create a fire that produces a lot of smoke for signaling purposes. This is achieved using green vegetation or materials that smoke rather than burn quickly. However, before you add these materials, you need to start with a strong, hot base fire. Use dry wood to establish this base, ensuring it's substantial enough to sustain the addition of green materials without being smothered.

Regarding signaling, the traditional method involves creating three fires in a triangle or straight line with about 100 feet (30 meters) between each fire. This arrangement is an internationally recognized distress signal, which can significantly increase your chances of being spotted by rescuers.

If you're in a situation where creating multiple fires isn't feasible, focus on producing the most smoke from a single fire. Once the base fire is hot and stable, add your green vegetation, rubber (if available), or any other material that produces thick smoke. The goal is to create a contrast against the background, with dark smoke being most visible against a light sky and vice versa.

Timing is also a critical factor in signaling with fire. If you're aware of search efforts or hear aircraft or rescue teams nearby, that's the time to maximize your fire's smoke output. Adding more smoldering materials can draw attention to your location during these periods.

Lastly, safety should never be compromised. Always ensure that your signal fire is manageable and that you have the means to extinguish it if necessary. The last thing you want is a signal fire to turn into a wildfire.

By mastering the skill of signaling with fire, you enhance your survival toolkit, preparing you for the unforeseen. Remember, the goal of wilderness survival is not just to endure but to emerge safely, and effective signaling is a critical component of that goal.

Extinguishing Fires Safely

After mastering the art of signaling with fire, it's equally crucial to understand how to extinguish fires safely and effectively. In the wilderness, managing your fire responsibly ensures your safety and preserving the natural environment around you. Here, we delve into practical techniques and considerations for safely putting out a campfire, a skill every outdoor enthusiast should have in their survival toolkit.

Firstly, planning is key. Always establish your fire in a clear, open space away from overhanging branches, dry grass, and other flammable materials. This precaution minimizes the risk of accidental spread. As your fire serves its purpose, whether for warmth, cooking, or signaling, begin the extinguishing process well before you intend to leave the site or retire for the night.

The most effective and immediate method to extinguish a fire is by using water. Douse your fire with ample water, ensuring that all embers, not just the flames, are thoroughly soaked. The goal is to cool all materials below their ignition point. However, simply throwing water on the fire isn't enough. Stir the ashes and embers with a stick or shovel to expose any hotspots hiding beneath the surface. Continue adding water and stirring until all hissing sounds cease, indicating the fire is out.

If water is scarce, which can often be the case in specific wilderness scenarios, sand or dirt can be an alternative solution. Cover the fire with a generous layer of sand or dirt to smother the flames. Just like with water, mixing and stirring the sand or dirt into the embers is essential to eliminate any hidden pockets of heat. Be cautious, as this method doesn't cool the fire as effectively as water. Ensure the fire is entirely out by feeling above the extinguished area for any heat emanating. If it's too hot to touch, it's too hot to leave.

Another vital aspect of fire extinguishment is timing. Never leave a fire unattended; ensure it's completely extinguished before leaving the site. A good rule of thumb is if it's too hot to touch, it's too hot to leave. This simple check can prevent forest fires and ensure you leave no trace of your presence in the wilderness.

Lastly, consider the environmental impact of your

actions. While water and sand are natural elements, excessive use can adversely affect the surrounding ecosystem. Use only as much water as necessary and avoid introducing large amounts of foreign materials like dirt or sand into a water source, which can disrupt aquatic life.

In conclusion, extinguishing fires safely in the wilderness is a fundamental skill that protects you and the environment. By employing these techniques, you ensure that your natural adventures are enjoyable and sustainable, leaving the wilderness as pristine as you found. Remember, a responsible outdoorsperson not only knows how to create fire but also how to extinguish it with care and consideration.

Chapter Summary

- Mastering firecraft is essential for wilderness survival, providing warmth, safety, and comfort.
- Selecting an appropriate site for a fire involves finding a sheltered, well-ventilated area and clearing it of debris.
- Fire requires three elements to thrive: heat, fuel, and oxygen, known as the "fire triangle."

- Gathering materials starts with tinder (easily ignitable materials), followed by kindling (small sticks) to build a flame, and finally, fuel wood (larger pieces) to sustain the fire.
- Assembling the fire typically involves creating a teepee structure with kindling around the tinder, allowing for good air circulation.
- Igniting the tinder can be done with matches, lighter, or primitive techniques, followed by gently blowing to provide oxygen and carefully adding larger pieces of wood.
- For signaling, a fire should be visible from a distance, using materials that produce a lot of smoke and, ideally, creating three fires in a recognizable distress pattern.
- Safely extinguishing a fire involves using water or sand to thoroughly soak or cover it, stirring to expose hotspots, and ensuring it's completely out before leaving.

4
FORAGING FOR FOOD

A group of people forage for food in the wilderness.

Identifying Edible Plants

In wilderness survival, the ability to identify edible plants can be a lifeline. Nature offers a bounty of nourishment, but it requires knowledge and caution to tap into this resource safely. This section delves into the essentials of recognizing plants that can sustain you in the wild.

First and foremost, familiarize yourself with the universal edibility test. This process, while time-consuming, is a valuable tool in determining whether a plant is safe to eat. It involves separating the plant into its essential components—leaves, stems, roots, and so on—and testing each part for edibility by applying a series of steps, including skin contact, tasting a small portion, and waiting for any adverse reactions. Remember, this test is a last resort and should only be used when unsure about a plant's edibility and have no other means of verification.

Knowledge of specific edible plants in the region you are exploring is invaluable. Many areas have unique flora, and what is edible in one place may not be found in another. Invest time in learning about the local vegetation before your adventure. Books, workshops, and guided tours can provide a wealth of information.

Some common edible plants found in various parts of the world include dandelions, whose leaves, flowers, and roots are edible; wild onions and garlic, identifiable by their distinctive smell; and cattails, found near freshwater sources, where the young shoots and roots can be consumed. Berries are also a potential food source, but caution is paramount as some are highly toxic.

Visual identification is crucial. Pay attention to the shape, size, color, and texture of leaves, flowers, and fruits. Many edible plants have poisonous look-alikes, so it's essential to note distinguishing features. For instance, wild carrots (also known as Queen Anne's lace) are edible but closely resemble the poisonous hemlock. The difference lies in the root's smell—wild carrots have a distinct carrot scent, while hemlock roots do not.

Tapping into local knowledge can be a game-changer. Indigenous peoples and local foragers possess generations of knowledge about the land and its resources. If you have the opportunity, learn from them. They can provide insights into which plants are edible and how to prepare them to neutralize toxins and enhance flavor.

In conclusion, foraging for food in the wilderness is both an art and a science. It requires patience, respect for nature, and a commitment to learning. By understanding the basics of plant identification and exercising caution, you can unlock the natural bounty that surrounds you. Remember, the key to successful foraging is knowing what you can eat and recognizing what you must avoid.

Avoiding Poisonous Plants

The bounty of nature offers a plethora of edible plants that can sustain you. But, it's equally important to be aware of the dangers lurking among those beneficial greens. Poisonous plants are not just a minor inconvenience; they can severely threaten your health and survival. This section aims to arm you with the knowledge to navigate the green wilderness safely, ensuring you can distinguish between nourishing sustenance and perilous flora.

First and foremost, familiarize yourself with the universal edibility test. This step-by-step process is a methodical way to determine the safety of a plant when you're unsure of its identity. It involves separating the plant into its essential components—leaves, stems, roots, and so on—and testing them one at a time for adverse reactions. While this test can be a lifesaver, it's time-consuming and should only be used as a last resort.

Knowledge is your best defense against poisonous plants. Before venturing into the wild:

1. Invest time in studying the region's flora.
2. Learn to identify not only the edible plants but also the poisonous ones.

3. Pay attention to details such as the shape of the leaves, the color of the berries, and the texture of the stems.

Books, apps, and local guides can be invaluable resources in this learning process.

Remember, some poisonous plants can mimic their edible counterparts, making them particularly dangerous. For instance, the deadly nightshade berry can easily be mistaken for an edible berry if one is not careful. Always err on caution; if you're unsure about a plant, it's better to leave it alone.

Another crucial tip is to avoid plants with telltale signs of toxicity. These include a bitter or soapy taste, milky or discolored sap, almond scent in woody parts and leaves, grain heads with pink, purplish, or black spurs, and three-leaved growth patterns. While these indicators are not foolproof, they warn that a plant may be harmful.

Lastly, consider the impact of your foraging. Avoid overharvesting and be mindful of the environment. Sustainable foraging ensures that the wilderness thrives and provides for future generations.

By equipping yourself with the knowledge to avoid poisonous plants, you safeguard your health and deepen your connection with nature. As you move on to mastering foraging techniques, remember that respect for the natural world and an understanding of its complexities are the foundations of successful wilderness survival.

Foraging Techniques

Embarking on the journey of foraging in the wilderness is not just about survival; it's about connecting with nature in its most primal form. However, to safely and effectively gather edible plants, nuts, fruits, and mushrooms, one must approach foraging with respect, knowledge, and practical techniques.

First and foremost, understanding the environment you're in is crucial. Different ecosystems offer varying bounties. For example, deciduous forests are rich in nuts and mushrooms, while coastal areas can provide seaweeds and shellfish. Begin your foraging adventure by researching the specific flora of your region.

Equipped with this knowledge, the next step is to familiarize yourself with the seasonal cycles of plants and fungi. Many edible plants have specific seasons when they are abundant, nutritious, and at their peak flavor. Learning these cycles ensures a successful forage and promotes sustainability by allowing plants to regenerate and complete their life cycles.

When you're out in the field, practice the "rule of three" - if you're unsure about the edibility of a plant, leave it. This rule is simple: Do not consume it if you cannot positively identify a plant and confirm it is edible from three separate, reliable sources. This cautious approach is a cornerstone of safe foraging.

Another technique is to start small. When trying a new plant for the first time, even if you're confident in its identification, consume a small amount and wait. Some plants can adversely affect specific individuals, so it's wise to ensure you don't react negatively.

Those looking to forage mushrooms have higher stakes due to the potential for poisonous look-alikes. Invest time in learning from experienced mushroom foragers or join local foraging groups. Many communities offer workshops or guided foraging walks. Remember, with mushrooms, when in doubt, throw it out.

Lastly, ethical foraging is as important as the techniques themselves. Always forage with sustainability in mind. Take only what you need, never deplete a single area of its resources, and be mindful of protected species and habitats. By foraging responsibly, you ensure these natural resources remain abundant for future generations.

As you transition from foraging to other means of wilderness sustenance, remember that the skills and respect for nature you've cultivated will serve you well. Whether gathering wild edibles or setting up traps for small game, sustainability, safety, and respect for the environment should always guide your actions.

Hunting and Trapping Small Game

The ability to secure food from your surroundings is paramount. While foraging for edible plants can sustain you, meat's nutritional value and energy can be a game-changer. This section delves into the essentials of hunting and trapping small game, a skill set that can significantly enhance your survival prospects.

The first step in hunting and trapping is understanding the small game available in your environment. Typical small game includes rabbits, squirrels, birds, and fish, depending on your location. Observing animal tracks, droppings, and feeding areas can give you insights into their habits and the best times to hunt or set traps.

Trapping is often more efficient than hunting, as it allows you to set multiple traps, increasing your chances of capturing game while you attend to other survival tasks. Here are a few simple yet effective traps:

1. **Snare Trap:** A snare is a looped wire or cord that tightens around an animal's neck or limb as it passes through. Position snares on known animal trails or near burrows. Check

them regularly to avoid leaving an animal trapped for too long.
2. **Deadfall Trap:** This trap uses a heavy weight, such as a rock or log, which falls and crushes the animal when it disturbs a trigger mechanism. Deadfalls require careful construction and placement to be effective and humane.
3. **Pitfall Trap:** Although more labor-intensive, a pitfall trap involves digging a deep hole to prevent the animal from escaping and covering it lightly with branches and leaves. It's particularly effective for larger rodents.

If trapping isn't an option, or you wish to actively hunt, creating improvised weapons can be your next course of action. A spear can be fashioned from a straight, sturdy stick, sharpened at one end, and hardened over a fire. Slingshots can be made with a Y-shaped branch and elastic material, suitable for small birds and rodents.

Always prioritize ethics and safety when hunting and trapping. Aim to kill quickly and humanely, minimizing suffering. Be aware of local regulations regarding hunting and trapping, and ensure you're not targeting endangered or protected species. Additionally, handle all animals with care to avoid injury and disease transmission.

Mastering the art of hunting and trapping small game can significantly bolster your food resources in a survival situation. By understanding animal behavior, employing simple trapping techniques, and improvising hunting tools, you can secure a vital source of nutrition. Remember, the key is in the capture and, ethically and safely, respecting the wilderness and its inhabitants.

Preparing Wild Food

Transitioning from the skills of hunting and trapping to the art of foraging, we delve into the world of preparing wild food. Foraging offers a sustainable way to supplement your diet with vitamins, minerals, and flavors often absent from the modern diet. However, the key to safely enjoying these natural bounties is proper identification, collection, and preparation.

Before you even think about eating a wild plant, identify it positively as edible. Many plants have poisonous look-alikes, so it's crucial to be 100% certain of their identity. Use reliable field guides, and learn from experienced foragers.

When collecting, choose young, tender leaves over older ones, as they are often more palatable and nutritious. Always forage away from polluted areas and roadsides to avoid contaminants. Remember, sustainability is vital: take only what you need and leave enough behind for the plant to thrive.

Once you've gathered your wild edibles, the next step is cleaning. Rinse your foraged goods thoroughly under running water to remove dirt, insects, or other debris. Some plants may require more specific preparation methods to make them safe or more palatable:

- **Boiling:** Certain wild greens, like dandelion leaves, can be bitter. Boiling them in water for a few minutes can help reduce their bitterness. Remember to change the water once or twice during boiling.
- **Soaking**: Some nuts and seeds contain tannins that can be removed by soaking them in water for several hours or overnight. This not only improves their flavor but also their digestibility.
- **Cooking:** Many wild foods, especially root vegetables, are best enjoyed cooked. Cooking not only makes them safer to eat by killing potential pathogens but also makes them easier to digest and their nutrients more accessible.

Incorporating wild foods into your diet doesn't have

to be complicated. Here are a couple of simple recipes to get you started:

- **Wild Berry and Nut Mix:** Forage for and wash wild berries, nuts, and edible leaves, ensuring they are safe to eat. Mix them for a nutritious wilderness snack.
- **Fire-Roasted Rabbit with Wild Herbs:** Season a cleaned wild rabbit with salt and freshly foraged herbs like rosemary and thyme, then roast over an open fire until cooked.

While foraging can enrich your diet and connect you with nature, safety should always be your top priority. Only eat something you're 100% sure about, and when trying a new wild food, start with a small amount to see how your body reacts. Remember, the wilderness is not a supermarket; it requires knowledge, respect, and a sense of responsibility.

By mastering the skills of foraging and preparing wild food, you add variety to your wilderness survival diet and deepen your connection with the natural world. The earth can provide abundant nourishment and pleasure with practice, patience, and respect for nature.

Chapter Summary

- Identifying edible plants is crucial for wilderness survival, offering a source of nourishment with knowledge and caution.
- The universal edibility test is a method to determine plant safety for consumption, involving skin contact, tasting, and waiting for reactions.
- Learning about local edible plants through books, workshops, and guided tours is invaluable, as edible flora varies by region.
- Common edible plants include dandelions, wild onions, garlic, cattails, and certain berries. However, caution is advised due to toxic look-alikes.
- Indigenous peoples and local foragers can provide deep insights into edible plants and their preparation to neutralize toxins and enhance flavor.
- Avoiding poisonous plants is critical; familiarize yourself with their characteristics and the universal edibility test to navigate safely.

- Foraging techniques emphasize respect for nature, knowledge of the environment, and ethical practices to ensure sustainability.
- Hunting and trapping small game, alongside foraging for plants, can significantly enhance survival prospects, requiring an understanding of animal behavior and ethical practices.

5

FIRST AID AND HEALTH

A woman and a man in the wilderness performing first aid on a broken leg.

Handling Bites and Stings

In the wilderness, where the beauty of nature meets the unpredictability of the wild, bites and stings can be a common occurrence. Whether it's a curious insect or a hidden snake, knowing how to handle these situations can be the difference between a minor inconvenience and a life-threatening emergency. This section delves into practical and effective methods to manage bites and stings, ensuring your adventure doesn't turn into a misadventure.

Immediate Actions for Insect Bites and Stings

The first step is to remain calm when dealing with insect bites or stings. Panic can accelerate the spread of venom in the body. If the stinger is still present, like bee stings, use a flat-edged object like a credit card to scrape it off. Avoid tweezers or squeezing it out, as this can inject more venom.

After removing the stinger, wash the area with soap and water to prevent infection. Applying a cold pack can reduce swelling and pain. However, ensure a barrier, like a cloth, between the ice and skin to avoid frostbite. For itching, a paste made from baking soda and water can offer relief when applied to the bite site.

Snake Bites

Snake bites, particularly from venomous species, require immediate and specific actions. The first rule is not to panic or attempt to suck out the venom, a common myth that can do more harm than good. Keep the affected limb immobilized and lower than the heart to slow venom spread. Do not apply a tourniquet or ice, which can cause further tissue damage.

Seeking professional medical help is crucial, even if unsure about the snake's venomous nature. While waiting for help, remove any jewelry or tight clothing near the bite area to allow for swelling. Remember, the goal is to keep the victim calm and still, reducing the heart rate and slowing the venom's spread.

Ticks

Ticks are masters of going unnoticed, making them particularly dangerous as they can transmit diseases. If you find a tick attached to your skin, use fine-tipped tweezers to grasp it as close to the skin's surface as possible. Pull upward with steady, even pressure. After removal, clean the bite area and your hands with rubbing alcohol, soap, and water.

Monitor the bite site for several weeks for any signs of rash or infection. Consult a healthcare provider immediately if you develop symptoms like fever, chills, or muscle aches.

Spiders

For spider bites, identification is critical. While most spider bites are harmless, those from a black widow or brown recluse spider require immediate medical attention. Symptoms of a dangerous spider bite can include severe pain, abdominal cramping, or a significant wound from tissue damage. If you suspect a bite from one of these spiders, apply ice to reduce swelling and seek medical help.

Prevention: Your Best Defense

While knowing how to handle bites and stings is essential, prevention remains the best strategy. Wear protective clothing, use insect repellent, and stay vigilant in environments where bites and stings are common. At night, use bed nets if sleeping in an exposed area. Always check your gear, clothing, and bedding for unwanted guests.

In conclusion, while the wilderness offers unparalleled experiences, it has risks. By understanding how to handle bites and stings effectively, you can ensure that your outdoor adventures remain safe and enjoyable.

Remember, the key is preparation, calmness, and swift action.

Natural Remedies

Did you know that nature can often provide its pharmacy in the wilderness? Understanding how to harness these natural remedies can be vital in managing health issues when you're far from conventional medical help. This section delves into natural remedies, offering practical advice on using the resources around you to maintain health and treat common ailments.

One of the most versatile plants you might encounter is the aloe vera. Known for its soothing properties, aloe vera gel can be applied to burns, cuts, and skin irritations, providing relief and promoting healing. If you have a sunburn or a minor kitchen burn while camping, look for an aloe plant, slice open a leaf, and apply the gel directly to the affected area.

Another invaluable natural remedy is activated charcoal from burnt wood or plant material. It's known for absorbing toxins, making it a valuable treatment for certain types of poisoning or stomach issues. If someone ingests a harmful substance, administering activated charcoal can help bind the toxin and prevent absorption by the body. However, it's crucial to seek professional medical advice as soon as possible in cases of poisoning.

For those dealing with insect bites or stings, plantain leaves, not to be confused with the banana-like fruit, can be a quick fix. These common weeds, often found in disturbed soils, have anti-inflammatory and wound-healing properties. Crushing and applying the leaves directly to the bite or sting can reduce pain and swelling.

Willow bark is another natural remedy with a long history of use. It contains salicin, a compound similar to aspirin, and can relieve pain, fever, and inflammation. You can chew on the raw bark or brew a tea to utilize willow bark. However, it's essential to correctly identify the willow tree and note that people allergic to aspirin should avoid using willow bark.

Lastly, for those navigating through stress or sleeplessness under the stars, consider the calming effects of chamomile. If you have chamomile tea bags, brewing a cup in the evening can help soothe nerves and promote a restful sleep. Chamomile flowers grow wild in many parts of the world. Still, it's essential to positively identify the plant before using it for tea to avoid consuming something potentially harmful.

While these natural remedies can relieve minor ailments and discomforts, they are not substitutes for professional medical treatment. Always prioritize safety and seek medical attention for serious injuries or conditions. However, utilizing these natural resources can enhance your self-reliance and comfort during your wilderness adventures.

Preventing and Treating Hypothermia and Heatstroke

Knowing how to prevent and treat hypothermia and heatstroke can distinguish between a memorable adventure and a life-threatening ordeal. These conditions represent the body's struggle to maintain its core temperature, battling the cold or the heat. Understanding the signs and knowing the immediate steps to take can save lives.

Hypothermia occurs when the body loses heat faster than it can produce it, causing the core body temperature to drop below 95°F (35°C). It can happen in temperatures as mild as 50°F (10°C) if a person is wet and exposed to wind. Prevention starts with layering clothing, focusing on materials that retain warmth even when wet, such as wool or synthetic fibers. Always keep the head and extremities covered, as a significant amount of body heat is lost through the head, hands, and feet.

Should you or a companion begin to show signs of hypothermia—shivering, slurred speech, clumsiness, confusion, or fatigue—it's crucial to act quickly. Move the person to shelter if possible. Replace any wet clothing with dry, warm layers. Share body heat by huddling close; if you have a sleeping bag, use it to trap warmth. Warm, sweet beverages can help increase the body's temperature, but avoid alcohol and caffeine, which can worsen the condition.

Conversely, heatstroke results from the body overheating, typically in temperatures above 90°F (32°C). It can occur due to prolonged exposure to high temperatures or physical exertion in hot weather. Prevention involves:

- Staying hydrated.
- Wearing light-colored and loose-fitting clothing.
- Avoiding strenuous activity during the hottest parts of the day.

Always be aware of the signs of heat exhaustion, which can precede heatstroke: heavy sweating, weakness, cold, pale and clammy skin, nausea, or vomiting.

If someone shows signs of heatstroke—high body temperature, hot and possibly dry skin, rapid pulse, headache, dizziness, nausea, confusion, or unconsciousness—immediate cooling is necessary. Move the person to a cooler place, remove excess clothing, and cool them down with whatever means available: a cool bath, wet cloths, or fanning. Hydration is critical, but only if the person is conscious and can swallow; give them water or sports drinks to sip slowly.

In both scenarios, monitoring the person closely and seeking medical attention as soon as possible is vital.

While these first aid measures can stabilize and improve the situation, professional medical help is essential to address these severe conditions fully.

Understanding these principles prepares you for the challenges of the wilderness. It equips you with the knowledge to help others in need. Remember, the wilderness demands respect, and part of that respect involves preparation and awareness of the risks, including the dangers posed by extreme temperatures.

Mental Health and Coping Mechanisms

It's easy to overlook the crucial aspect of mental health. Yet, maintaining mental and emotional well-being is as vital as addressing physical injuries or environmental threats like hypothermia and heatstroke. This section delves into practical coping mechanisms and strategies to ensure your mental resilience matches your physical endurance when facing the unpredictability of the wild.

The first step in managing your mental health in a survival situation is recognizing the body's natural stress responses: fight, flight, or freeze. These reactions are your body's way of preparing to face a threat. However, in a prolonged survival situation, these responses can become your biggest adversaries if not correctly managed. Recognizing the signs of stress in yourself—such as increased heart rate, rapid breathing, and difficulty focusing—can help you take early steps to mitigate their impact.

One of the most effective ways to control stress and anxiety in the wilderness is through controlled breathing techniques. For instance, the "4-7-8" technique involves breathing in for 4 seconds, holding the breath for 7 seconds, and exhaling slowly for 8 seconds. This method helps reduce anxiety and can bring your focus back to the present, making tackling the task at hand easier.

In a survival situation, it's easy to become overwhelmed by what you're facing. To maintain mental clarity and a sense of progress, break down your survival tasks into small, manageable goals. Whether it's building a shelter, finding water, or simply making it through the next hour, focusing on one task at a time can help keep feelings of despair at bay and provide a sense of accomplishment.

Establishing a routine can provide a sense of normalcy and control in an otherwise unpredictable environment. Simple tasks, like setting up and breaking down camp at the exact times each day, can offer comfort and a sense of order. This routine can also ensure that essential tasks are noticed in the stress of the moment.

Maintaining a positive outlook is crucial for mental endurance. This doesn't mean ignoring the reality of your situation but rather focusing on what you can control and finding reasons to be hopeful. Celebrate your successes, no matter how small, and remind yourself of your strengths and capabilities.

If you're not alone, lean on the social support available. Sharing feelings, offering encouragement, and working together towards common goals can significantly boost morale and reduce the psychological burden of survival.

Engaging in mental exercises like visualization, meditation, or even simple games can distract you from stressors and improve your mood. Visualization can be compelling; imagining a successful outcome or recalling a happy memory can provide a mental escape and renew your determination.

Surviving in the wilderness requires a holistic approach that includes physical survival skills and strategies for maintaining mental health. Understanding and managing stress responses, employing practical coping mechanisms, and fostering a positive, goal-oriented mindset can significantly improve your resilience in adversity. Remember, the wilderness may test you, but it can also reveal untapped wells of mental and emotional strength.

Chapter Summary

- Encounters with wildlife and insects in the wilderness can lead to bites and stings, some of which may be serious if not treated properly.
- For insect stings, it's essential to remove the stinger quickly without squeezing it, clean the area, and apply ice to reduce swelling.
- Snake bites should not be treated with myths like sucking out venom; instead, immobilize the limb and seek medical help immediately.
- Spider bites from dangerous species like black widows or brown recluses require immediate medical attention for symptoms like severe pain or tissue damage.
- To remove tick bites, use fine-tipped tweezers, clean the area, and monitor for signs of diseases like Lyme disease.
- Prevention of bites and stings includes wearing protective clothing, using insect repellent, and staying vigilant in risky environments.

- Natural remedies in the wilderness include aloe vera for burns, activated charcoal for poisoning, and plantain leaves for insect bites.
- Managing mental health in the wilderness involves recognizing stress responses, employing breathing techniques, setting small goals, maintaining a routine, staying positive, seeking social support, and engaging in mental exercises.

6
SURVIVAL GEAR ESSENTIALS

A backpacker holding a compass.

The Survival Kit

In wilderness survival, your kit is not just a collection of items but your lifeline. It's essential to understand that the effectiveness of your survival kit hinges not just on what you include but on how well each tool serves its purpose. This brings us to a critical aspect of wilderness preparedness: choosing the right tools for your survival kit.

The cornerstone of selecting the right tools lies in understanding the environment you're venturing into and the challenges you might face. A desert explorer's kit will differ vastly from that of a mountaineer or a jungle trekker. However, specific tools have universal utility, regardless of the terrain.

Firstly, a high-quality, multi-purpose knife is indispensable. It serves numerous survival needs, from preparing food to crafting shelter. The choice between a fixed blade and a folding knife often comes down to personal preference and the specific demands of your adventure. Fixed blades are generally more durable and reliable for heavy-duty tasks while folding knives offer convenience and portability.

Next, a reliable fire starter is crucial. Options range from waterproof matches and lighters to magnesium fire starters and ferro rods. Each has advantages, but having at least two different types in your kit can prepare you for varying conditions. Remember, the ability to start a fire can mean the difference between life and death in the wilderness, providing warmth, light, and a means to cook food and purify water.

Navigation tools are also vital. While technology has given us GPS devices and smartphones, these can fail or run out of power. A traditional compass and waterproof map of the area you're exploring should always be part of your kit. Understanding how to use these tools effectively before you embark on your journey is just as important as having them.

Water purification methods are another critical component. Whether you opt for purification tablets, a portable filter, or a UV light purifier, ensure you can make natural water sources safe to drink. Dehydration can quickly become a severe threat to survival, making water purification a top priority.

Lastly, a first aid kit tailored to your specific needs and the nature of your adventure should always be noticed. Include personal medications, bandages, antiseptic wipes, and other needed items in an emergency. The contents of your first aid kit should reflect the activities you're undertaking and the potential injuries you might encounter.

Choosing the right tools for your survival kit is about balancing the need for versatility, reliability, and weight. Each item should serve multiple purposes and be tested and familiar to you before setting out. Remember, your survival kit is your best friend in the wilderness – choose its contents wisely.

Choosing the Right Tools

The gear you carry can mean the difference between a manageable and dire situation. After understanding the basics of what constitutes a comprehensive survival kit, the next crucial step is discerning which tools are essential for your specific needs and how to select them wisely. This section delves into choosing the right tools for your wilderness adventures, ensuring you're well-equipped for whatever nature throws your way.

First and foremost, prioritize multi-purpose tools. Space and weight are at a premium in any pack, and each item you carry should serve multiple functions. A classic example is a Swiss Army knife or a multi-tool, which combines several tools in one compact package. Look for items that can fulfill multiple purposes, such as a hatchet that can be used for chopping wood and hammering.

Durability is another crucial factor. Your survival gear should be able to withstand the rigors of the outdoors. This means opting for items made from high-quality materials that are known for their strength and longevity. Stainless steel tools, for example, resist rust and endure harsh conditions, making them a wise choice for any survival kit.

Consider the environment you'll be venturing into as well. Different terrains and climates require different tools. For instance, a water purifier is indispensable in areas with uncertain access to clean water. At the same time, a sturdy pair of snowshoes is essential for traversing snowy landscapes. Tailor your gear to the specific challenges and resources of the environment you'll be exploring.

Ease of use is another critical consideration. In a survival situation, you want tools that are straightforward and reliable. Complex gadgets may seem appealing, but in high-stress scenarios, simplicity often prevails. Choose tools that you can operate efficiently, even under pressure.

Lastly, educate yourself on the use of each tool in your kit. Owning a high-quality survival tool is only beneficial if you know how to use it effectively. Take the time to practice and become proficient with each piece of equipment before you find yourself in a survival situation.

As we transition from understanding the foundational elements of a survival kit to exploring the possibilities of creating your gear, remember that the tools you carry are as much about personal preference as practicality. The right tools for you are those that align with your skills, your environment, and your survival strategy. With careful selection and a bit of know-how, you can assemble a kit that not only enhances your wilderness experience but could also save your life.

DIY Survival Gear

Having the right gear can mean the difference between a minor inconvenience and a life-threatening situation. However, only some have the budget or access to high-end survival gear. This is where ingenuity and some DIY skills come in handy. By creating your own survival gear, you save money and gain a deeper understanding of how each piece functions, which can be invaluable in a survival scenario.

One of the most versatile and essential pieces of survival gear is a multi-purpose tool. While commercial versions are available, you can create a basic version using items you likely already have at home. Start with a sturdy pocketknife, the cornerstone of your DIY multi-tool. You can add a mini flashlight, a small fire starter kit (which can be as simple as a few matches and a striker), and a compact signal mirror. These items can be bundled with a strong rubber band or encased in a handmade pouch. The key is to ensure that your DIY multi-tool is compact enough to carry easily but comprehensive enough to be useful in various survival situations.

Another critical piece of survival gear is a water filtration system. Clean drinking water is paramount, and while boiling water is an effective method to purify it, having a portable filtration system can be a lifesaver. A simple DIY water filter can be made using a small plastic bottle, cotton cloth, charcoal, sand, and gravel. By layering these materials in the bottle, you create a basic but effective filtration system that can remove particulates and improve the taste of water from natural sources.

Shelter is another vital aspect of wilderness survival. While nothing can entirely replace a high-quality tent, there are ways to improvise in an emergency. One of the most straightforward DIY shelters is a tarp shelter. With a durable tarp, some paracord, and a little know-how, you can create a variety of shelters to protect yourself from the elements. The key to a successful tarp shelter is choosing the right location and ensuring it is securely anchored. This can be achieved by tying your paracord to trees or using rocks and logs to weigh down the tarp's edges.

Lastly, always appreciate the importance of an excellent first aid kit. While many items in a commercial kit can be purchased individually, you can supplement it with DIY alternatives. For example, duct tape can be used in place of medical tape for securing bandages, and a clean cotton shirt can be torn into strips for use as gauze. Additionally, familiarizing yourself with natural remedies and medicinal plants can enhance your DIY first aid kit and provide you with more options in a wilderness survival situation.

Creating your survival gear equips you with the tools

you need to face the wilderness and instills confidence and self-reliance. Remember, the goal of DIY survival gear is not to replace high-quality commercial equipment but to complement it and provide alternatives when necessary. As you become more proficient in crafting your gear, you'll find that your ability to adapt and overcome in the wilderness will grow exponentially.

Maintaining Your Gear

Your gear is not just a set of tools—it's your lifeline. Thus, maintaining your survival gear is as crucial as having it in the first place. This section delves into practical strategies to ensure your equipment remains in top condition, ready to serve its purpose when you need it most.

Firstly, regular inspection of your gear is non-negotiable. Before and after each wilderness excursion, take the time to check each item thoroughly for signs of wear and tear. Look for damage that could compromise the item's functionality, such as cracks in water containers, fraying on rope ends or dullness in knife blades. Early detection of potential issues allows for timely repairs or replacements, preventing equipment failure in critical moments.

Cleaning your gear is equally important. Dirt, grime, and moisture can degrade materials, reducing their effectiveness and lifespan. After every use, clean your tools according to the manufacturer's instructions. For example, wash and dry metal items to prevent rust, air out sleeping bags and tents to avoid mildew, and clean filters in water purification devices to ensure optimal performance.

Proper storage is another critical aspect of gear maintenance. Store your equipment in a cool, dry place away from direct sunlight and extreme temperatures, which can cause materials to deteriorate. Keep sharp objects safely sheathed and place electronics in waterproof containers to protect them from moisture. Organizing your gear thoughtfully also means you can access it quickly when preparing for your next adventure.

Repairing your gear is a skill that every wilderness enthusiast should cultivate. Familiarize yourself with basic repair techniques, such as patching holes in fabric, fixing broken buckles, and sharpening blades. A well-stocked repair kit, including items like duct tape, sewing materials, and multi-purpose glue, can be a game-changer in extending the life of your gear.

Lastly, upgrading your gear is an ongoing process. While maintaining your equipment can significantly extend its usability, there comes a time when replacement or upgrade becomes necessary. Stay informed about advancements in survival gear technology and consider how new items could enhance your wilderness experience. However, always weigh the benefits of new gear against the familiarity and reliability of your existing equipment.

In conclusion, maintaining your survival gear requires a proactive approach, encompassing regular inspection, cleaning, proper storage, repair, and thoughtful upgrading. By dedicating time and effort to care for your equipment, you ensure that it remains reliable, functional, and ready to support you in your wilderness adventures. Remember, the condition of your gear can make the difference between thriving and merely surviving in the great outdoors.

Innovative Uses for Common Items

As we delve into wilderness survival, we must recognize that the most ordinary items can transform into indispensable tools under dire circumstances. This section explores the innovative uses for standard items, turning everyday objects into survival gear essentials.

Dental Floss: Beyond its primary dental hygiene use, it is solid and versatile. It can be used as a fishing line, a snare for small game, or to tie together shelter materials. Its compact size and lightweight nature make it an unassuming yet valuable addition to any survival kit.

Aluminum Foil: Often overlooked, aluminum foil is a multifaceted tool in survival situations. It can be molded into a container to boil water, used as a reflective signal for rescue, or fashioned into a makeshift fishing lure. Wrapping it around your body or shelter can help retain heat during cold nights.

Sanitary Pads: While it might seem unconventional, sanitary pads are highly absorbent and sterile, making them excellent for first aid purposes, such as dressing wounds. They can also be used as fire starters; the cotton material catches fire quickly, especially when separated into thinner layers.

Plastic Bags: These ubiquitous items can serve multiple purposes in the wilderness. A clear plastic bag can be used for solar water disinfection (SODIS), where the sun's UV rays purify water. Plastic bags can also collect rainwater or as a waterproofing layer for keeping essential items dry.

Condoms: Despite their intended use, condoms have properties that make them surprisingly useful for survival. They can hold a significant amount of water, making them useful for storage. They are also stretchable and can be used as makeshift rubber bands for securing or bundling items.

Chapstick: Beyond moisturizing lips, Chapstick can be a valuable tool in survival scenarios. The wax can be used to waterproof small items or to lubricate zippers and other gear. Combined with a cotton ball, it can also serve as a productive fire starter.

Eyeglasses: If you wear eyeglasses, they can be more than just a vision aid. In sunny conditions, the lenses can focus sunlight to start a fire. This method requires patience and precision but can be a lifesaver when matches or lighters are unavailable.

Steel Wool: Commonly used for cleaning, steel wool can also be a vital survival tool. When touched by the terminals of a battery, it can ignite and serve as a fire starter. This is particularly useful in damp conditions where traditional methods may fail.

By reimagining the uses of these everyday items, you can significantly enhance your survival toolkit without adding bulk or excessive weight. This approach prepares you for unexpected situations and encourages creativity and resourcefulness in the wilderness. Remember, the most ordinary items can become extraordinary tools in survival scenarios.

Chapter Summary

- Understanding the environment and challenges ahead is crucial for selecting the right tools for a survival kit, with some tools having universal utility.
- A high-quality, multi-purpose knife and a reliable fire starter are indispensable in any

survival kit for tasks like preparing food and starting fires.
- Navigation tools, such as a traditional compass and waterproof map, are vital, especially when technology fails.
- Water purification methods are essential to make natural water sources safe to drink, highlighting the importance of hydration in survival situations.
- A tailored first aid kit should address specific needs and potential injuries, including personal medications and emergency items.
- The selection of survival gear should prioritize multi-purpose tools, durability, and suitability for the specific environment and challenges.
- DIY survival gear, like an essential multi-tool or a simple water filtration system, can be a cost-effective and educational approach to preparedness.
- Regular inspection, cleaning, proper storage, repair, and thoughtful gear upgrading are essential for maintaining survival equipment.

7
WATER CROSSINGS AND TRAVEL

A dangerous river crossing.

Crossing Rivers Safely

Crossing rivers in the wilderness demands a careful approach, combining caution, knowledge, and sometimes courage. The decision on how and whether to cross is crucial for safety. Here are vital tips and techniques for safely navigating this aspect of wilderness travel.

Before attempting to cross, thoroughly assess the river, considering its width, depth, and current speed. Swollen rivers from recent rains or snowmelt may necessitate waiting or finding another route, as water above knee height can sweep you off your feet, and fast-moving water poses a danger even if shallow.

Choosing the right spot to cross is essential. Look for a straight section of the river where you can consistently assess flow and depth, avoiding bends where the outer side is often more profound and faster. Areas where the river widens, indicating shallower and slower water or places with visible rocks or sandbars are preferable for crossing.

Preparation involves loosening backpack straps for easy removal if you fall while keeping it on for potential buoyancy. Secure loose items and waterproof essential gear. Use a sturdy stick or trekking pole for stability and to probe the water ahead.

When crossing, face upstream, leaning into the current to maintain balance, and move sideways with small, shuffling steps, keeping your feet on the riverbed. Avoid crossing directly or downstream to reduce slipping or being pushed over risks. If in a group, crossing together can offer additional stability.

Recognizing when a river is too dangerous to cross is crucial. If in doubt, it's safer to turn back or wait for conditions to improve, prioritizing safety over progress.

Adhering to these guidelines enhances the likelihood of a safe river crossing. However, each river and situation is unique, necessitating judgment and opting for the safest choice when uncertain. Successfully crossing a river may lead to further challenges, such as building rafts or floats for larger bodies of water or impassable obstacles, requiring adaptation and different survival skills.

Building Rafts and Floats

The ability to traverse water bodies safely and effectively can be a matter of survival in the wilderness. After understanding the principles of crossing rivers safely, it's equally crucial to grasp the basics of constructing rafts and floats, especially when swimming or wading isn't viable due to the water's depth, current strength, or temperature.

Building a raft or float requires ingenuity and understanding basic buoyancy principles. The first step is to scout for materials that can float. Deadwood, dried reeds, and bundles of lighter branches are excellent starting points. In some environments, you may also find buoyant materials like empty plastic bottles or foam pieces, which can be repurposed effectively.

The construction of a raft hinges on creating a stable platform. Begin by laying out two longer logs parallel to each other, which will serve as the base of your raft. These should be thick enough to support your weight and the weight of any gear you need to transport. Across these, tie shorter logs or branches to form the raft's deck. Use vines, strips of bark, or even sturdy grasses as rope, ensuring each piece is securely fastened to prevent your raft from coming apart mid-crossing.

For floats, the approach is slightly different. If you're in a pinch, tying a bundle of light branches or reeds together can create a makeshift floatation device. This won't offer a raft's stability or carrying capacity but can be a quick solution to keep you buoyant. Similarly, if you've managed to find or salvage plastic bottles, securing them together in a net or with rope can create an effective float. This method is beneficial for supporting your weight while swimming across a body of water.

Testing is a critical next step before committing to your crossing. Place your raft or float into the water near the shore and gradually apply weight to assess its buoyancy and stability. It's better to discover any weaknesses while you're still within easy reach of land.

Remember, the goal of using a raft or float is not speed but safety. Once you're on the water, maintain a low center of gravity to avoid capsizing. Use a long stick or branch as a makeshift paddle to help guide your raft or assist in swimming with your float.

In constructing these survival aids, creativity and resourcefulness are your best tools. Each situation may call for a different approach based on the materials at hand and the specific challenges of the water body you're facing. With practice and patience, building rafts and floats can become a valuable skill in your wilderness survival toolkit, bridging the gap between the shores of uncertainty and the land of safety.

Swimming in Open Water

Swimming in open water can be daunting, especially when you are in a wilderness survival situation. However, you can navigate these waters safely and efficiently with the proper knowledge and techniques. This section will guide you through the essential tips and strategies for swimming in open water, ensuring you're prepared for whatever challenges you face.

First and foremost, it's crucial to assess the water conditions before diving in. Look for currents, obstacles, and any signs of wildlife that could pose a threat. If the water is running fast, consider looking for a narrower section where the speed might decrease, or use natural barriers to your advantage to cross safely.

When it comes to swimming technique, conserving energy is critical. Use a relaxed, steady stroke to maintain a consistent pace without exhausting yourself. The breaststroke and sidestroke are particularly effective for this purpose, as they provide good buoyancy and visibility. Keep your movements as smooth and flat as possible to reduce drag and make swimming easier.

Buoyancy aids can be a lifesaver in open water. If you're crossing a long distance, having something that helps you float can conserve energy and provide a sense of security. If available, this could be a life jacket or improvised flotation devices made from materials at hand, such as sealed plastic bags filled with air or foam pieces.

Navigation is another critical aspect of swimming in open water. Always have a clear destination and use landmarks to guide your way. Use the sun or stars to maintain your direction if visibility is low. Swimming parallel to the shore is also wise when possible, providing a reference point and a quick escape route if needed.

Lastly, always appreciate the importance of staying calm. Panic is your worst enemy in survival situations, especially in open water. Maintain a positive mindset, focus on breathing, and keep a steady pace. Remember, your mental resilience is just as important as your physical endurance.

By following these guidelines, you can navigate open waters with confidence. Remember, preparation and knowledge are your best tools for wilderness survival. Stay informed, stay calm, and you'll be well-equipped to handle whatever comes your way.

Dealing with Marine Hazards

Navigating through wilderness water bodies requires a keen understanding of marine environments' challenges and potential hazards. Dealing with these hazards effectively ensures safety and success in wilderness survival. This includes practical strategies and tips for handling situations during water crossings and travel.

When crossing rivers, streams, or coastal areas, one of the most significant risks comes from the force of moving water. Currents can be surprisingly strong, and tides can quickly change the depth and intensity of water bodies. To safely navigate these, it's essential to assess the water from the shore before attempting to cross, looking for signs of solid currents or a noticeable pull. Planning your crossing during low tide can make the water calmer and shallower for tides. If caught in a strong current, swimming parallel to the shore until you can escape the current's pull and then angling back towards the shore is advised.

Submerged logs, rocks, and vegetation are severe

threats to travelers, potentially trapping or injuring you. Since clear visibility is rare in wilderness settings, moving cautiously and using a stick or pole to probe the water ahead can help identify obstacles. It's crucial to move slowly and ensure a firm footing before advancing.

Encounters with marine life, ranging from leeches in freshwater to jellyfish in saltwater, can vary from being nuisances to posing severe dangers. Wearing clothing or a wet suit to cover as much skin as possible in areas known for harmful marine life can minimize risks. In areas with jellyfish, dragging a stick through the water ahead of you can help deter them. Seeking first aid immediately after encountering potentially harmful marine life is essential for addressing any injuries or adverse reactions.

Hypothermia is a risk even in warm climates, especially during crossings in cold rivers or lakes. Keeping crossings brief and having dry clothes ready to change immediately afterward can protect against hypothermia. If crossing in a group, doing so together can provide additional warmth and stability against currents.

Water quality is another concern, as polluted or stagnant water can harbor bacteria and parasites harmful to humans. It's important to avoid ingesting water during crossings and to clean any part of your body that comes into contact with suspicious water as soon as possible.

Being prepared and knowledgeable about these marine hazards can significantly reduce the risks associated with water crossings and travel in the wilderness. Caution, preparation, and respect for the power of nature are vital principles for successful navigation, setting you on the path to mastering safe and efficient water crossings.

Conserving Energy During Travel

Mastering the art of energy conservation during travel, especially after navigating through marine hazards, is crucial. The transition from water crossings to continued travel on land demands a strategic approach to preserve your strength and resources. Here, we delve into practical hacks to conserve energy, ensuring you remain robust and ready to face the challenges ahead.

Firstly, it's essential to understand the principle of pacing. Unlike a sprint, survival is a marathon. After dealing with the unpredictability of water, your body needs to recover even as you move. Adopt a pace that allows you to breathe easily and speak in complete sentences. This pace might seem slow, but it's sustainable, ensuring you can cover more ground without overexerting yourself.

Secondly, the importance of planning must be balanced. Before embarking on the next leg of your journey, take a moment to assess your route. Look for paths that offer the least resistance. Dense underbrush, steep inclines, and rocky terrains are energy zappers. Whenever possible, choose flat, clear paths. Utilize natural landmarks to navigate, reducing the need for constant map checks or GPS usage, which can mentally drain you.

Hydration and nutrition play pivotal roles in energy conservation. Your body functions best when adequately fueled. After a water crossing, replenish any lost fluids and electrolytes. Snack on high-energy, nutrient-dense foods that are easy to digest. Foods like nuts, dried fruits, and energy bars offer a quick energy boost without the sluggishness of heavier meals.

Another hack lies in the art of layering your clothing. Conditions can change rapidly, and managing your body temperature is critical to conserving energy. Wet clothes can lead to hypothermia, even in mild conditions, draining your energy reserves. Change into dry clothes if available, or wring out wet garments to remove excess water. Dress in layers that can be easily adjusted to prevent overheating or chilling.

Lastly, rest is as important as movement. Short, strategic breaks can significantly boost your endurance. Find a comfortable spot to sit or lie down, elevate your feet to reduce swelling, and take deep breaths to lower your heart rate. Even a 10-minute rest can rejuvenate your body and mind, making the next stretch of your journey more manageable.

In conclusion, transitioning from water crossings to land travel in a survival situation requires a mindful approach to energy conservation. You can significantly enhance your endurance and overall survival by pacing yourself, planning your route, managing your nutrition and hydration, dressing appropriately, and incorporating rest. Remember, in the wilderness, wise energy use is just as important as the distance you cover.

Chapter Summary

- Crossing rivers safely involves assessing the river's width, depth, and current speed and sometimes waiting for conditions to improve or finding an alternative route.
- Ideal crossing points are straight river sections, avoiding bends and looking for shallower, slower areas with visible rocks or sandbars for support.
- Preparation for crossing includes loosening backpack straps for quick release if needed, securing loose items, and using a stick or trekking pole for stability.

- Proper crossing involves facing upstream, leaning into the current, and moving sideways with small shuffling steps, with group crossings offering added stability.
- Knowing when to turn back is crucial, prioritizing safety over progress if the river seems too dangerous.
- Building rafts and floats from materials like deadwood, dried reeds, or plastic bottles can aid in crossing deeper or stronger currents, with stability and buoyancy testing essential before use.
- Swimming in open water requires assessing conditions, using energy-conserving strokes like breaststroke or sidestroke, utilizing buoyancy aids, navigating with landmarks or celestial bodies, and staying calm.
- Dealing with marine hazards includes understanding how to navigate currents and tides, avoiding underwater obstacles, protecting against harmful marine life, preventing hypothermia, and ensuring water quality, with energy conservation strategies like pacing, route planning, proper nutrition and hydration, layering clothing, and resting effectively for continued travel on land.

8
WEATHER AND ENVIRONMENT

Rainy weather in the wilderness.

Predicting Weather Patterns

Understanding and predicting weather patterns becomes a crucial survival skill in the heart of the wilderness. The ability to read the sky, the behavior of animals, and the patterns of nature can mean the difference between being prepared for a sudden storm and being caught off guard. This section delves into traditional and modern methods to forecast weather, ensuring you can adapt to your environment effectively.

One of the most accessible indicators of impending weather changes is the sky. Cloud formations, in particular, can tell us much about what to expect. For instance, high, wispy cirrus clouds often indicate fair weather. Still, their gradual accumulation can suggest a change is on the horizon, usually indicating that a storm system may be moving in. With their towering presence, Cumulonimbus clouds are a clear signal of thunderstorms and potentially severe weather. Identifying these and other cloud types can give you a heads-up hours or days in advance.

Another traditional method of predicting weather involves observing animal behavior. Many animals are susceptible to changes in air pressure and can behave differently as weather systems approach. Birds flying lower than usual can indicate bad weather ahead, as they try to avoid the discomfort of flying in lower pressures that precede storms. Frogs are known to croak louder and more frequently when bad weather is on the way, a survival instinct tied to their breeding patterns.

The behavior of plants can also offer clues about the

weather. For example, some flowers close their petals in anticipation of rain. Pine cones open up in dry weather and close in moist weather due to the expansion and contraction of their scales in response to humidity.

In addition to these natural indicators, modern technology has given us tools that can aid in weather prediction. Portable weather radios provide updates and warnings, invaluable in areas prone to sudden weather changes. Smartphone apps can offer real-time weather data and forecasts. However, it's important to remember that you may only sometimes have a signal in remote wilderness areas.

Understanding these signs and signals requires patience and practice. It's a skill to develop over time through observation and experience. By paying attention to the sky, wildlife, and plant life and using available technology, you can become adept at predicting weather patterns. This knowledge enriches your outdoor experience and enhances your ability to stay safe in the wilderness.

As we move forward, it's crucial to remember that predicting the weather is just one aspect of dealing with environmental challenges. The next step is learning how to survive and thrive in the extreme conditions that nature can throw our way. Your ability to adapt and utilize survival strategies will be tested, whether in extreme heat or cold.

Surviving in Extreme Conditions

Conditions can quickly change from safe to dangerous, requiring physical strength, environmental knowledge, and quick adaptation. This discussion focuses on essential survival techniques that could mean the difference between life and death in nature's extreme situations.

Finding or creating shelter is a top priority in harsh conditions. The shelter provides necessary shade in intense heat, while in cold environments, it offers warmth and protection from the wind. While natural shelters like caves can be lifesavers, often you'll need to build your own. In snowy conditions, igloos or snow caves can keep you warm and block the wind, and in forests, lean-tos constructed from branches and leaves can protect you from rain and sun. The goal is to utilize what the environment offers to make your shelter as sturdy and insulated as possible.

Dealing with extreme heat involves managing the risk of dehydration and heatstroke. It's vital to find and purify water, with boiling being the most reliable method. However, solar stills can work in dry areas. Wearing loose, light-colored clothing helps prevent heatstroke, and it's essential to stay shaded and cover your head and neck during peak sun hours.

In cold settings, staying hydrated is equally

challenging, and it's safer to melt snow or ice before consuming to avoid lowering your body temperature. Avoiding alcohol and caffeine is wise, as they can dehydrate you. Staying warm involves layering clothes, staying dry, recognizing signs of hypothermia and frostbite, ensuring extremities are protected, and avoiding tight clothing that restricts blood flow.

Finding food becomes crucial in extreme conditions as your body needs more energy. Knowing local flora and fauna can transform a seemingly barren area into a food source. Fish and game can be plentiful in colder climates, but you must know how to trap or fish. Knowing which plants are edible and how to forage in warmer climates efficiently can save your life.

Navigating through extreme terrains requires careful planning and energy conservation. Knowing how to make and use snowshoes or safely traverse glaciers is essential in snowy or icy conditions. Using the sun, stars, or natural landmarks in deserts or jungles can prevent getting lost in vast, featureless areas.

Surviving in extreme conditions is as much a mental challenge as a physical one. Overcoming fear, loneliness, and uncertainty is crucial. Keeping a positive attitude, setting achievable goals, and staying busy can help combat despair. Survival is more than just enduring; it's about adapting and thriving despite adversity.

In summary, surviving extreme conditions demands

knowledge, preparation, and adaptability. Understanding the environment, utilizing available resources, and maintaining a resilient mindset are critical to overcoming the challenges of the harshest environments. As we move forward, the ability to adapt to various environments underscores the importance of versatility and ingenuity in wilderness survival.

Adapting to Different Environments

The environment around you can be as unpredictable as beautiful. Adapting to different environments is not just about survival; it's about understanding the natural world and how to coexist. Whether you find yourself in dense forests, arid deserts, icy tundras, or along coastlines, each setting requires unique skills and knowledge to navigate successfully.

In dense forests, the canopy provides shelter, limits visibility, and makes navigation challenging. To adapt, focus on learning how to read the natural signs for direction—moss growth, sun position, and the behavior of water streams can guide you. Building a shelter in such an environment often means utilizing the abundant materials around you, like branches and leaves, to create insulation and protection from the elements.

Deserts present a stark contrast, where water scarcity and extreme temperature fluctuations are often the primary concern. In these environments, conserving energy and moisture becomes paramount. Travel during the cooler hours of the early morning or late evening to avoid the harshest heat. Use clothing to shield your skin from the sun and retain moisture. Finding water may require knowledge of extracting moisture from plants or locating hidden sources underground.

The cold is relentless in icy tundras, and the landscape may seem barren. However, snow and ice can be both a challenge and a resource. Building a snow shelter can protect you from the wind and insulate against the cold. Understanding how to move safely across the ice, recognizing signs of hypothermia, and finding food sources are critical skills. Fire-making is essential, not just for warmth but for melting snow for water.

Coastal environments offer a bounty of resources but also unique hazards. Learning how to source fresh water, either through collection methods or by identifying freshwater streams, is crucial. The sea can provide food, but knowledge of local marine life and tides is necessary to avoid danger. Shelter might need to account for changing tides and the potential for damp conditions.

In each of these environments, the principles of survival remain constant: find shelter, water, and food and maintain a positive mental attitude. However, the methods by which you achieve these needs can vary dramatically. Adapting to different environments is about flexibility, observation, and a willingness to learn from the natural world. It's about making the environment work for you, using its resources wisely, and respecting its limits.

As we move forward, remember that protecting yourself from the elements is not just about immediate survival. It's about planning, preparation, and understanding the nuanced interplay between the weather and your environment. Whether it's the scorching sun, the pouring rain, or the biting cold, each element presents challenges and opportunities for the knowledgeable survivor.

Impact of Climate Change on Survival

The elements are not just a backdrop to our adventures; they are dynamic forces that shape our experiences, challenge our skills, and test our resilience. As the planet warms, the impact of climate change on these natural elements becomes increasingly significant, altering the very fabric of wilderness survival. Understanding these changes is not just about staying ahead in the survival game; it's about adapting to a rapidly changing world where the rules of engagement with nature are constantly rewritten.

Climate change has led to more extreme weather

patterns, including increased temperatures, intense storms, and unpredictable weather events. These changes affect the environment and the strategies needed for survival in the wilderness. For instance, higher temperatures can lead to dehydration and heatstroke, making water sourcing and cooling techniques paramount. Meanwhile, the increased frequency and intensity of storms demand improved shelter-building skills and the ability to predict weather changes accurately.

Moreover, climate change impacts the availability and distribution of resources. Shifts in climate zones affect the habitats of plants and animals, altering the availability of food and materials in certain areas. For example, as temperatures rise, some plant species that survivalists might rely on for food or medicine are moving to higher elevations or latitudes. Similarly, animal migration patterns are changing, affecting hunting and trapping. Adapting to these shifts requires a deeper understanding of local ecosystems and the flexibility to adjust traditional survival techniques.

The melting of snow and ice is another critical aspect of climate change affecting wilderness survival. In regions where ice fishing, snow shelter construction, or glacier navigation were once standard survival practices, the changing conditions demand new skills and knowledge. For instance, thinner ice presents new dangers for crossing frozen lakes, requiring more sophisticated techniques to assess ice safety.

Rising sea levels and the increased acidity of oceans and freshwater sources pose additional challenges, especially in coastal areas. Saltwater intrusion can make finding potable water more complex, and the changing composition of aquatic ecosystems can affect the availability of fish and other marine resources.

To navigate these challenges, survivalists must become students of the environment, continuously learning and adapting. This means honing traditional survival skills and integrating new knowledge about climate change and its effects. It involves staying informed about the latest scientific findings, understanding the local impacts of global changes, and developing a versatile skill set that can be adapted to various conditions.

In conclusion, the impact of climate change on wilderness survival is profound and multifaceted. It challenges us to rethink our strategies and adapt our skills to a changing world. By embracing this challenge, we can become more resilient, resourceful, and in tune with the natural world, ensuring that we can thrive in the wilderness, no matter what the future holds.

Chapter Summary

- Understanding and predicting weather patterns, involving traditional methods and modern technology, is crucial for survival in the wilderness.
- Cloud formations, animal behavior, and plant reactions indicate impending weather changes.
- Modern tools like portable weather radios and smartphone apps aid in weather prediction. However, their effectiveness can be limited in remote areas.
- Survival in extreme conditions requires knowledge of shelter construction, hydration management, and food sourcing specific to the environment.
- Psychological resilience and physical preparation are crucial in surviving harsh conditions.
- Adapting to different environments (forests, deserts, tundras, coastlines) requires unique skills and knowledge for each setting.
- Protecting oneself from the elements involves creating shelters, understanding wind, harnessing fire, layering for temperature

regulation, staying dry, sun protection, and hydration strategies.

- Climate change impacts wilderness survival by altering weather patterns and resource availability and requiring new survival strategies and adaptability to changing conditions.

9

SURVIVAL PSYCHOLOGY

Three adventurers surviving in the wild.

Staying Calm Under Pressure

In the wilderness, the unexpected is the only guarantee. You might feel immense pressure rapidly if faced with a sudden storm, a lost path, or dwindling supplies. In these moments, when the stakes are highest, staying calm under pressure becomes your most crucial survival skill. This section delves into practical strategies to maintain composure and make rational decisions, even when every instinct might be urging you to panic.

First and foremost, acknowledge your feelings. Fear, anxiety, and stress are natural responses to threatening situations. Recognizing these emotions without judgment allows you to assess them objectively and prevents them from overwhelming your thought process. Remember, your goal is not to eliminate these feelings but to manage them effectively.

Breathing techniques are a powerful tool in regaining control over your emotional state. Deep, controlled breaths can help reduce stress levels and improve cognitive function. Remember the "4-7-8" technique from Chapter 5?

1. Inhale deeply through your nose for 4 seconds.
2. Hold your breath for 7 seconds.
3. Exhale slowly through your mouth for 8 seconds.

This method calms the nervous system and

encourages a moment of pause to assess your situation more clearly.

Visualization is another effective strategy. Imagine yourself successfully navigating the challenge at hand. This not only boosts confidence but also helps in formulating a practical plan of action. Visualization primes the brain for success, making you more likely to achieve the outcome you're focusing on.

Maintaining a positive attitude is crucial. It's easy to spiral into despair when faced with adversity, but positivity can be a powerful motivator. Focus on what you can control rather than what you can't. Celebrate small victories, no matter how minor they may seem. These moments of success build momentum and reinforce your belief in overcoming obstacles.

Lastly, prioritize tasks to avoid feeling overwhelmed. Break down your situation into manageable actions. Ask yourself, "What's the most important thing I need to do right now?" By focusing on one task at a time, you can maintain a sense of control and progress, which is essential for staying calm under pressure.

In wilderness survival, as in life, staying calm under pressure can make the difference between success and failure. By mastering these techniques, you equip yourself with the mental resilience to face any challenge head-on. Remember, the wilderness does not discriminate; it is unforgiving to panic but rewarding to preparedness and composure.

The Will to Survive

The will to survive becomes a psychological concept and a tangible force that can mean the difference between life and death. This section delves into the essence of this will, exploring how it shapes our actions, decisions, and, ultimately, our survival in the wild.

Survival psychology posits that the will to survive is intrinsic to human nature, yet it manifests differently in each individual. It's a complex interplay of mental, emotional, and physical factors that can be nurtured and strengthened over time. Understanding and harnessing this will is crucial for anyone battling the elements, far from the comforts and safety of civilization.

One of the first steps in cultivating a strong will to survive is recognizing the power of positive thinking. In adversity, the mind can be your greatest ally or worst enemy. Negative thoughts can spiral into despair, panic, or resignation, which can hasten defeat. Conversely, maintaining a positive outlook can inspire creativity, resilience, and the determination to overcome obstacles. It's about focusing on one's goals, not the hurdles, and believing in one's ability to prevail.

Another critical aspect is motivation. This can come

from the desire to reunite with loved ones, the responsibility to provide for a family or even the personal challenge of testing one's limits. Identifying this motivation is crucial, as it serves as a beacon of hope, a constant reminder of why it's essential to keep pushing forward, even when the situation seems impossible.

Preparation and knowledge also play significant roles in strengthening the will to survive. The more skilled and informed one is about survival techniques, the more confident and mentally prepared one will be when facing challenges. This confidence boosts morale and fosters a proactive attitude, essential for survival. It's about transforming fear into focus, channeling energy into constructive actions rather than allowing panic to consume and immobilize.

Adaptability is another critical component. The wilderness is ever-changing, and survival often hinges on adapting to new challenges and environments. This requires flexibility in thinking, the willingness to learn from mistakes, and the creativity to devise novel solutions. It's a testament to the human spirit's capacity to endure and evolve in adversity.

Lastly, the will to survive is deeply connected to the human instinct for connection and support. Even in solitude, the thought of loved ones or the prospect of returning to them can provide immense psychological strength. In group situations, collective will and mutual support can amplify individual efforts, creating a powerful synergy that enhances the chances of survival for everyone involved.

In conclusion, the will to survive is a multifaceted force shaped by mindset, motivation, preparation, adaptability, and human connection. It's about harnessing the power of the mind, body, and spirit to face the unknown with courage, determination, and hope. As we move forward, understanding how to make decisions in crises becomes the next critical step, building on the foundation of a strong will to survive.

Decision-Making in Crisis Situations

Every decision can mean the difference between survival and peril. When faced with a crisis, making sound, timely decisions becomes paramount. This section delves into the critical aspects of decision-making in crises, offering practical advice to navigate the complexities of survival psychology.

First and foremost, it's essential to maintain a calm demeanor. Panic is the archenemy of rational decision-making. When you find yourself in a crisis, take a deep breath and assess your situation with as much objectivity as possible. This moment of pause allows your brain to switch from reactive to proactive, enabling you to evaluate your options more clearly.

Next, prioritize your needs. In a survival situation, your primary concerns should be shelter, water, fire, and food, in that order. This hierarchy of needs can guide your decision-making process, helping you focus on what's most critical at any given moment. For instance, if you're lost in a cold environment, finding or creating shelter to protect yourself from the elements becomes your top priority.

Another critical aspect of decision-making in the wilderness is gathering information. Before making any decisions, try to collect as much data about your surroundings and situation as possible. This could involve observing the sun's position to determine direction, checking your supplies to know what you have at your disposal, or scouting your immediate area for resources or hazards. Armed with this information, you can make more informed decisions that increase your chances of survival.

Setting realistic goals and breaking them down into manageable tasks is also crucial. Instead of fixating on the end goal of being rescued, focus on what you can achieve right now. Whether building a shelter, starting a fire, or signaling for help, each small victory can boost your morale and propel you forward.

Lastly, be prepared to adapt. The wilderness is unpredictable, and what works in one situation may not work in another. Flexibility and the willingness to change your plan as new information becomes available are vital components of effective decision-making in crises.

Understanding and applying these principles can enhance your ability to make sound decisions when it matters most. Remember, your mind is your most valuable survival tool in the wilderness. Cultivating strong decision-making skills can help you navigate the challenges of the wild but also enrich your everyday life with greater resilience and adaptability.

Group Dynamics and Leadership

The psychological aspect of survival often becomes as crucial as the practical skills of finding shelter, water, and food. Within this realm of survival psychology, understanding group dynamics and leadership can significantly influence the outcome of a survival situation. This section delves into the intricacies of how groups function in extreme conditions and the pivotal role of leadership in navigating the challenges that arise.

When individuals are in a survival scenario as part of a group, the initial reaction can range from panic to denial. During these first moments, the foundation for group dynamics is laid. A group's ability to organize, allocate resources, and make collective decisions can mean the difference between despair and hope. The key to this organization often lies in the emergence of leadership.

Leadership in a wilderness survival context only sometimes follows conventional norms. The most physically strong or vocally assertive individual is only sometimes the best leader. Instead, effective leadership often emerges from those who can maintain calm, think clearly under pressure, and possess relevant survival skills. A leader's ability to inspire confidence, foster cooperation, and maintain morale becomes their most valuable asset.

However, leadership is more than just one person taking charge. It also involves recognizing the strengths and weaknesses within the group and delegating tasks accordingly. A leader who can empower others to contribute meaningfully optimizes the group's chances of survival and helps maintain a positive group dynamic. This collaborative approach can prevent conflict and ensure that decisions are made considering the group's best interests.

Communication plays a critical role in maintaining effective group dynamics. In the silence of the wilderness, transparent and open communication can prevent misunderstandings and ensure that everyone is aware of the group's plans and objectives. A leader must facilitate this communication, encouraging everyone to voice their thoughts and concerns. This inclusivity can bolster group cohesion and resilience in the face of adversity.

Yet, leadership in survival situations has its challenges. The stress and strain of the environment can lead to tension and conflict within the group. A leader must navigate these interpersonal dynamics with sensitivity and assertiveness, addressing issues before they escalate and threaten the group's unity. It is a delicate balance between maintaining authority and fostering mutual respect.

In conclusion, the dynamics of group behavior and the essence of leadership in wilderness survival are complex and multifaceted. A group's ability to organize itself, with a leader who can effectively harness its collective strengths, significantly enhances its survival prospects. As we move forward, understanding the psychological underpinnings of these dynamics can equip individuals with the knowledge to face the wilderness not just as a collection of individuals but as a unified entity with a shared goal of survival. This understanding of group dynamics and leadership serves as a bridge to navigating the emotional and psychological challenges posed by isolation and fear, further emphasizing the interconnectedness of survival psychology.

Coping with Isolation and Fear

In the wilderness, the challenges extend beyond the physical to include significant psychological hurdles, such as dealing with isolation and fear. These emotions can become overwhelming, mainly when separated from their group or alone in an unfamiliar setting. However, learning to manage these feelings is crucial for survival. Here are several effective strategies for overcoming the psychological challenges of isolation and fear.

Accepting your situation is the first step toward overcoming any challenge. Recognize and accept your feelings of fear and isolation without judgment, understanding that it's a natural response to uncertainty. This acceptance allows you to focus on constructive actions rather than being immobilized by fear.

Keeping busy is essential. An idle mind can exacerbate fear and negative thoughts, so engage in survival-related tasks such as building a shelter, gathering food, or creating signals for rescue. These activities improve your chances of survival and give you a sense of purpose and accomplishment, which can be uplifting in difficult times.

Establishing a routine can introduce a sense of normalcy to your situation. Set specific times for various tasks, including foraging, resting, and shelter maintenance. This structure helps maintain focus and reduces feelings of aimlessness and despair.

Mindfulness and meditation are powerful tools for managing fear and anxiety. Dedicate time each day to sit quietly, breathe deeply, and observe your surroundings without judgment. This practice can ground you in the present moment, alleviating feelings of isolation and fear.

Visualization of positive outcomes, a technique widely used by athletes and successful individuals, can also be beneficial. Regularly imagine yourself being rescued or finding your way back to safety. These positive visualizations can enhance morale and motivation, keeping spirits high even in challenging situations.

Connecting with nature can also provide comfort. While isolation can be challenging, it offers a unique opportunity to connect with the natural world. Appreciate the beauty around you, whether it's the sound of a stream, the sight of wildlife, or the sun's warmth. This connection can create a sense of belonging and peace, reducing feelings of loneliness.

Keeping a journal allows you to express your thoughts and experiences constructively. Documenting your journey can offer valuable insights and remind you of your resilience and strength.

Most importantly, maintain hope. Remember why

you're striving to survive and the loved ones awaiting your return. Hope is a powerful motivator that can drive you to persevere through the most challenging times.

Addressing the mind and body is essential when coping with isolation and fear in the wilderness. By implementing these strategies, you can preserve your psychological well-being, significantly improving your chances of survival. Survival is as much about mental resilience as it is about physical endurance.

Chapter Summary

- Acknowledge feelings of fear and anxiety without judgment to manage them effectively and prevent them from overwhelming your thought process.
- Use breathing techniques, like the "4-7-8" method, to reduce stress and improve cognitive function, helping to maintain composure in stressful situations.
- Employ visualization to boost confidence and formulate practical action plans, priming the brain for success.
- Maintain a positive attitude, focusing on controllable aspects and celebrating small

victories to build momentum and belief in overcoming obstacles.
- Prioritize tasks to avoid feeling overwhelmed, breaking down situations into manageable actions to maintain control and progress.
- Cultivate a solid will to survive by focusing on positive thinking, identifying motivation, preparing with knowledge, adapting to changes, and valuing human connections.
- Enhance decision-making skills in crisis by staying calm, prioritizing needs, gathering information, setting realistic goals, and being prepared to adapt.
- Navigate group dynamics and leadership in survival situations by organizing, utilizing effective communication, recognizing individual strengths, and maintaining group cohesion and morale.

10
ADVANCED SURVIVAL TECHNIQUES

An explorer creating a fireplace.

Improvised Weapons and Tools

Creating improvised weapons and tools from the natural environment can be a critical survival skill in the wilderness. This section delves into the art of crafting essential tools and weapons using only what nature provides, ensuring you're prepared for both the challenges of survival and the necessity of self-defense.

Crafting Improvised Weapons

1. **Spears:** A spear can be made by sharpening a long, straight stick. A rock or bone can be shaped and attached to the tip for a more durable point. Spears are helpful for hunting and can serve as a defensive weapon against predators.
2. **Slingshots:** A Y-shaped branch, coupled with a rubber band or tire's inner tube, can be transformed into a slingshot. Small rocks or metal pieces serve as effective ammunition. This weapon is handy for small-game hunting.
3. **Bows and Arrows:** Crafting a bow and arrow requires more time and skill but is highly effective for hunting from a distance. Flexible wood, string, and feathered arrows are the components of this classic survival weapon.

Creating Essential Tools

1. **Knives:** A sharp stone, flint, or even a piece of bone can be fashioned into a cutting tool. These improvised knives are crucial for preparing food, crafting other tools, and various survival tasks.
2. **Axes:** A larger stone attached to a sturdy stick can serve as an improvised axe. This tool is invaluable for chopping wood for fire or shelter construction.
3. **Fishing Gear:** You can assemble adequate fishing gear using natural fibers to create a line and shape bone or wood into hooks. Additionally, nets can be woven from vines or plant fibers.

Maintenance and Safety

Maintaining your improvised weapons and tools is essential to remain functional and practical. Regular inspection is crucial in identifying any wear and tear or damage that could compromise their performance. By dedicating time to repair and upkeep, you can extend the lifespan of your equipment, ensuring it is ready and reliable when you need it most. This proactive maintenance approach saves resources and ensures that your tools and weapons perform optimally.

Safety should always be prioritized when handling

and storing improvised weapons and tools. It is essential to familiarize yourself with the proper handling techniques for each piece of equipment. This includes understanding how to safely use, transport, and store them to minimize the risk of accidental injury to yourself or others. Implementing safe practices can prevent unnecessary accidents and ensure that your tools and weapons are preserved in good condition for future use.

In addition to regular maintenance and practicing safe handling, creating a designated storage area for your tools and weapons can further enhance safety. This area should be secure, organized, and, ideally, accessible only to those trained and authorized to use the equipment. By keeping your tools and weapons in a designated area, you reduce the risk of them being mishandled or used by untrained individuals. This organized approach not only contributes to the overall safety of your environment but also helps maintain the condition and readiness of your equipment.

In conclusion, mastering the art of creating improvised weapons and tools is a testament to human ingenuity and adaptability. These skills enhance your chances of survival and deepen your connection with the natural world. As you progress in your wilderness survival journey, remember that the environment around you is rich with resources—each with the potential to aid your survival.

Constructing Long-Term Shelters

Mastering the construction of long-term shelters is a crucial skill in wilderness survival, going beyond the basics of creating a temporary refuge. This involves understanding the specific environment, as different climates and terrains necessitate different shelter types. For example, a dense forest environment would benefit from the abundant wood for construction. In contrast, a desert environment would require a focus on insulation and shade.

The first step in building a long-term shelter is selecting an appropriate site. It's essential to find a flat, well-drained area sheltered from prevailing winds and close to a water source yet not prone to flooding. The site should also be safe from hazards like falling branches or wildlife paths.

The materials for the shelter depend on what's available in the surroundings. In wooded areas, fallen branches, leaves, and moss are helpful, while in more barren landscapes, rocks, earth, and any repurposable human-made materials might be necessary. Tools can range from simple knives or hatchets to more sophisticated tools brought with or improvised from the environment.

Constructing a long-term shelter typically starts with building a sturdy frame from larger branches or logs, using lashing techniques with vines or makeshift ropes for security. Insulating the walls and roof with materials like leaves, grass, or snow is crucial, and the entrance should be positioned away from the wind. Incorporating a fireplace or stove can provide warmth.

For a shelter to be sustainable long-term, it must be sturdy and capable of being repaired and improved over time. Enhancing insulation, ensuring proper drainage, and constructing simple furniture can make the shelter more comfortable.

Safety is paramount, with regular maintenance to check for wear and tear, safe management of fire, and cleanliness to deter wildlife being critical practices.

Constructing a long-term shelter in the wilderness is an advanced skill that requires patience, ingenuity, and a comprehensive understanding of the environment. By carefully selecting the site, utilizing available materials wisely, and focusing on sustainability and safety, it's possible to create a refuge that protects from the elements and offers a comfortable living space in the wild.

Advanced Navigation Challenges

Navigating the wilderness with precision and safety is an essential skill distinguishing between a successful journey and getting lost. This guide explores advanced navigation challenges encountered in the wild and how to tackle them using traditional and modern techniques. These methods are crucial for survival and enhance the outdoor experience by fostering a deeper connection with nature.

A topographical map is an invaluable tool in the wilderness, detailing the area's physical features, including elevations. Learning how to read contour lines, identify landmarks, and understand the map's scale is essential. Combining this knowledge with a compass enables confident navigation through unfamiliar terrain. Practicing triangulation, which involves identifying three known locations on your map and using your compass to find the bearings from your current location to these points, is a critical skill, especially when GPS is not an option.

When a compass is unavailable, the natural environment offers alternative navigation aids. The sun's path, star movements, and even tree moss growth patterns can indicate direction. For example, in the Northern Hemisphere, the sun rises in the east and sets in the west, with noon in the southern sky. At night, the North Star (Polaris) points north. These natural cues help maintain a general sense of direction.

While traditional navigation skills are indispensable, modern technology like GPS devices and satellite messengers can enhance navigation and safety. However, using these tools judiciously is crucial, ensuring spare batteries or power sources are at hand and not relying solely on technology, as devices can fail or lose signal.

Different environments present unique navigation challenges. Dense forests, steep terrains, and vast deserts each require tailored strategies. For instance, dense forests limit visibility and make landmarks harder to spot, necessitating close attention to maps and compasses and using short, precise journey segments to stay oriented. In contrast, deserts offer long-distance visibility of landmarks, though distances can be deceptive due to clear air. Accurately estimating distances and using the sun's position are crucial to desert navigation.

Developing a mental map and maintaining situational awareness is also vital. This involves continuously observing the environment, noting landmarks, and mentally updating your position. Anticipating potential hazards and planning routes accordingly is part of this proactive navigation approach, keeping you oriented and enhancing your wilderness experience.

Mastering these advanced navigation challenges prepares you to explore the wilderness safely and confidently. Whether employing a map and compass, utilizing natural indicators, or integrating modern technology, preparation and practice are essential. Navigation is about reaching your destination and understanding and connecting with the natural world around you.

Living Off the Land

The ability to live off the land is a fundamental skill that ensures sustenance and fosters a deeper connection with nature. As we build on our advanced navigation skills, we rely on the natural resources around us for survival. This guide is designed to provide you with practical and innovative strategies to make the most of the wilderness's bounty.

To start, developing a thorough understanding of your surroundings is crucial. Different ecosystems, from forests and mountains to deserts and coastal areas, offer a variety of resources for survival. Each environment has its unique set of plants, animals, and other materials that can be used for food, water, and shelter. An essential field guide to the local flora and fauna can be invaluable.

Foraging for food is a crucial survival skill, requiring both knowledge and caution. It's essential to distinguish between edible and toxic plants, and familiarizing yourself with the universal edibility test can help determine the safety of unknown plants. Besides plants, insects and small game can also provide nutrition. Techniques such as setting snares or fishing with improvised gear can be effective. Still, being aware of local regulations and ethical considerations is essential.

Water is a critical resource, and finding a reliable source is a top priority. Natural formations that collect rainwater, streams, or even morning dew on vegetation can be water sources. However, any water found must be purified to prevent waterborne diseases, with boiling being the most effective method. Solar water disinfection (SODIS) or makeshift filters can also be used without fire-making tools.

Building a shelter is crucial for protection against the elements. The type of shelter will depend on the available resources and environmental conditions, ranging from lean-tos made of branches to snow caves. The shelter should be sturdy, insulated from the cold ground, and offer protection from the elements.

As you hone your skills in living off the land, it's important to practice sustainability. Taking only what you need, respecting wildlife, and leaving no trace are principles that ensure the preservation of the environment and the availability of resources for future survival needs.

Integrating these survival skills with your knowledge of navigation and self-rescue prepares you for a comprehensive survival strategy, enabling you to thrive in the wilderness. Remember, adaptability is critical. The land provides us with the tools for survival; it's our responsibility to learn how to use them effectively. With practice, patience, and respect for nature, living off the land can become a means of survival and a rewarding way of life.

Self-Rescue Strategies

Exploring the essentials of living off the land is crucial. Still, it's equally important to understand the strategies that could save your life if lost or stranded in the wilderness. Self-rescue strategies go beyond merely finding your way back to civilization; they involve making informed decisions to increase your chances of survival and rescue. These strategies are considered advanced not because they require special skills but because they demand higher awareness, preparation, and mental fortitude.

Making yourself visible to rescuers is a critical first step in self-rescue. This can be achieved by using both natural and human-made materials to create signals that are visible or audible from a distance. Placing brightly colored clothing or materials in open areas, using mirrors or any reflective surface to catch the sun's rays, and lighting fires at night can all serve as effective signals. It's important to remember that three of anything, such as fires, blasts on a whistle, or flashes of light, is universally recognized as a distress signal.

Basic navigation skills can mean the difference between aimlessly wandering and moving towards safety. It's beneficial to know how to use a compass and maps. Still, in their absence, natural indicators like the sun's position, the movement of stars, and the growth patterns of moss on trees can guide you. The goal is to move purposefully and conserve energy for the journey ahead.

Suppose you're near a body of water. In that case, constructing a makeshift raft or learning to navigate rivers can significantly improve your mobility and chances of being found, as water bodies often lead to populated areas. However, it's essential to be aware of the risks, including hypothermia and swift currents.

Leaving markers or a trail for rescuers to follow can also increase your chances of being found. This can be done by tying pieces of fabric to branches, stacking rocks, or drawing arrows in the dirt, aiming to leave a clear path to your current location.

In some situations, the best strategy might be to stay put, especially if you're injured, have limited mobility, or are in an area that meets your basic needs. In such cases, making your location visible and conserving energy are crucial and focusing your signaling efforts to ensure rescuers can find you.

Psychological resilience is the most critical aspect of self-rescue. The will to survive, staying calm under pressure, and the determination to keep going against the odds ultimately define a survivor. Mindfulness and stress management techniques can help maintain a clear head and a hopeful heart.

In the wilderness, every decision can significantly impact your survival. By employing these self-rescue strategies, you're actively participating in your survival, not just waiting to be found. With the proper knowledge and mindset, you can navigate out of challenging situations and back to safety.

Chapter Summary

- Crafting improvised weapons like spears, slingshots, bows, and arrows can be essential for hunting and self-defense in the wilderness.
- Essential tools such as knives, axes, and fishing gear can be made from natural materials for survival tasks like food preparation and shelter construction.
- Regular maintenance and safe handling of improvised weapons and tools are crucial to ensure their functionality and prevent accidents.
- Constructing long-term shelters requires understanding the environment, selecting a

suitable site, and using available materials for construction and insulation.
- Advanced navigation challenges in the wilderness can be tackled using traditional methods like maps and compasses, natural indicators, and modern technology.
- Living off the land involves foraging, hunting, finding water, and building shelters with sustainability and respect for nature in mind.
- Self-rescue strategies include making oneself visible to rescuers, navigating purposefully, leaving markers, and maintaining psychological resilience.
- The skills to create improvised tools, navigate challenging terrains, live sustainably off the land, and execute self-rescue strategies are vital for wilderness survival.

THE JOURNEY AHEAD

A survivalist in the wilderness.

Reflecting on What We've Learned

As we pause to reflect on the journey we've embarked upon together, we must recognize the breadth and depth of knowledge we've explored in the realm of wilderness survival. Our exploration has been comprehensive and enlightening, from the foundational skills necessary for any outdoor adventure to the advanced techniques that could mean the difference between life and death in extreme situations.

In traversing this vast landscape of survival wisdom, we've equipped ourselves with practical hacks and strategies and fostered a deeper appreciation for the natural world and our place within it. The skills we've discussed are not merely tools for survival; they are invitations to engage more fully with the environment, to understand its rhythms and nuances, and to respect its power and beauty.

The journey of learning is, by its very nature, unending. Each experience in the wilderness offers new lessons, and each challenge faced provides opportunities for growth and reflection. The knowledge we've acquired is a solid foundation, but it is just the beginning. The actual test of our understanding comes not from mastering the techniques in theory but from applying them in the unpredictable and often unforgiving theater of the great outdoors.

As we move forward, it's crucial to remain curious, open-minded, and willing to continue our education in wilderness survival. The landscape of survival knowledge is as dynamic as the environments it pertains to, with new insights, techniques, and technologies constantly emerging. Staying informed about these developments is a matter of personal interest and a fundamental aspect of responsible wilderness exploration.

Moreover, practicing these skills in real-life scenarios, whether during planned expeditions or unexpected situations, will refine our abilities and deepen our understanding. Each outing is an opportunity to test our knowledge, assess our preparedness, and learn from our successes and setbacks.

In embracing continuous learning, we also open ourselves to the broader community of wilderness enthusiasts and survival experts. Sharing experiences, exchanging tips, and learning from others' perspectives enrich our understanding and contribute to a collective pool of knowledge that benefits all who venture into the natural world.

As we look ahead, let us carry forward the spirit of resilience, adaptability, and respect for nature that has guided our journey thus far. The path of wilderness survival is as much about personal growth and connection with the environment as it is about overcoming challenges. By continuing to educate ourselves and embrace the lessons the wilderness has to teach, we ensure that our adventures are safe, successful, and deeply rewarding.

Continuing Your Survival Education

It's crucial to recognize that the learning journey is only partially complete. The wilderness, with its ever-changing landscapes and unpredictable challenges, demands a continuous commitment to education and skill enhancement. Embracing this ongoing learning process is not just about survival; it's about thriving in the most unexpected circumstances.

Continuing your survival education means seeking new knowledge, techniques, and experiences. The world of wilderness survival is vast, encompassing various environments, each with unique challenges and secrets. From the dense, humid rainforests to the arid expanses of deserts, every environment offers lessons waiting to be learned.

One effective way to continue your education is through practical experience. Regularly put yourself in new and challenging situations within safe and controlled parameters. Whether it's a weekend spent practicing navigation in a local forest or a planned expedition in a more demanding environment, each experience builds upon the last, deepening your understanding and honing your skills.

Another invaluable resource is the knowledge in books, online courses, and workshops. The perspectives and experiences of other survivalists can offer insights that might take years to learn on your own. Diversify your sources of information to include a broad spectrum of environments and survival philosophies. Remember, there's always something new to learn, and someone else's experiences can illuminate aspects of survival you might not have considered.

Engaging with a mentor can also significantly accelerate your learning curve. A mentor with a wealth of experience and knowledge can offer personalized guidance, helping you navigate the complexities of wilderness survival more efficiently. They can provide feedback on your techniques, suggest areas for improvement, and share wisdom that only comes from years of direct experience.

Lastly, embracing the mindset of a lifelong learner is the most crucial aspect of continuing your survival education. Stay curious, open-minded, and willing to leave your comfort zone. The wilderness is a great teacher, offering lessons in resilience, adaptability, and the sheer beauty of the natural world. By committing to an ongoing learning journey, you ensure that you're not just prepared to survive but equipped to thrive, no matter what challenges the wilderness may present.

As we move forward, remember that the wilderness

survival community is a vibrant and supportive network eager to welcome new members. Engaging with this community enriches your survival skills. It contributes to the collective knowledge and resilience of those who share your passion for the great outdoors.

Joining the Survivalist Community

As you've journeyed through the realm of wilderness survival, acquiring skills and knowledge to navigate the unpredictable embrace of nature, you're now standing at a pivotal crossroads. Your path has been one of self-discovery, resilience, and an ever-deepening connection with the natural world. Yet, the journey doesn't end here. It's time to consider how you can continue to grow and prepare for your own adventures and contribute to and benefit from a larger community of like-minded individuals. This is where joining the survivalist community comes into play.

The survivalist community is a vibrant and diverse network of individuals who share a common passion for wilderness survival, self-sufficiency, and a profound respect for nature. By becoming part of this community, you open doors to a wealth of knowledge, experience, and camaraderie that can enrich your survival skills and deepen your appreciation for the wild.

Engaging with the survivalist community can take

many forms. Online forums and social media groups offer a platform to connect with fellow enthusiasts from around the globe. Here, you can share your own experiences, learn from others' adventures and misadventures, and find answers to questions you might not have even known to ask. These digital spaces are treasure troves of information where the community's collective wisdom is just a few clicks away.

Local clubs and organizations provide another avenue to immerse yourself in the survivalist culture. Participating in workshops, meetups, and expeditions can offer hands-on experience and the opportunity to forge real-world connections with individuals who share your interests. These interactions can be invaluable, providing mentorship, friendship, and the chance to learn and practice skills in a supportive environment.

Moreover, joining the survivalist community isn't just about what you can learn from others; it's also about what you can contribute. Your unique experiences, insights, and skills are valuable to the community. Whether sharing a novel survival hack you've discovered, offering advice based on your personal experiences, or volunteering to lead a workshop, your contributions can help others on their survival journey.

As you consider joining the survivalist community, remember that it's a step towards enhancing your survival skills and building a more resilient, knowledgeable, and connected network of wilderness enthusiasts. It's about being part of something larger than yourself. This community values the lessons learned in the embrace of nature. It is committed to preserving and respecting the wild spaces that inspire us all.

So, as you prepare for your next adventure, think about how you can engage with the survivalist community. Whether through online platforms, local groups, or even starting your initiative, your participation can enrich your wilderness journey in ways you've yet to imagine. The path ahead is not just about surviving; it's about thriving, learning, and sharing in the collective wisdom of a community that shares your passion for the wild.

Preparing for Your Next Adventure

Standing on the brink of your next wilderness adventure, it's essential to recognize that thorough preparation is the cornerstone of surviving and thriving in the great outdoors. The journey you're about to embark on requires as much mental and physical readiness as it does enthusiasm for the unpredictability of nature. Consider these vital tips to ensure you're well-prepared for whatever challenges you might face.

Firstly, commit to continuous learning. The realm of wilderness survival is broad and constantly changing.

Keep yourself updated with the latest survival techniques, gear advancements, and environmental changes by reading books, taking online courses, and attending workshops. This ongoing education will keep your survival knowledge up-to-date.

Next, make sure to inspect and update your gear before you leave. Check your tools, shelter, sleeping equipment, and the expiration dates on your first aid supplies and food. This is also an excellent time to consider investing in new gear to enhance your safety and comfort during your adventure.

Physical preparation cannot be overlooked. Wilderness survival demands a lot from your body, so regular exercise that improves cardiovascular health, strength, and flexibility is crucial. Design your fitness routine to reflect the activities you'll be doing, such as hiking, climbing, or paddling, to prepare your body for the challenges ahead better.

Mental resilience is the most critical aspect of your preparation. The wilderness can be as mentally taxing as it is physically—practice stress management techniques like mindfulness or meditation to bolster your mental toughness. Being calm and thinking clearly under pressure can significantly impact your survival.

Gaining practical experience is invaluable. Test your skills in controlled settings by participating in survival workshops, joining outdoor clubs, or planning short trips.

These experiences are excellent teachers, providing insights and building confidence that only come from practice.

Always have a detailed plan for your adventure, including your route, expected return times, and backup plans. It's equally important to inform someone you trust about your plans so that they know where to look for you if something goes wrong.

Lastly, embrace the survivalist mindset, which emphasizes adaptability, resilience, and a profound respect for nature. Approach each adventure with humility and an eagerness to learn from the environment and your experiences.

As you gear up for your next wilderness journey, remember that it's not just about testing your survival skills but also about forging a deeper connection with nature, discovering your strengths, and pushing beyond your limits. With the proper preparation, you're not merely surviving; you're thriving, learning, and evolving into a more skilled and resilient adventurer with each step you take into the wild.

Final Thoughts

As we draw the curtains on this guide, we must reflect on what we've journeyed through together. The wilderness, with its untamed beauty and unpredictable challenges, is a profound metaphor for life. Each survival hack, tip, and anecdote shared within these pages is more than just a means to endure the physical world; they are lessons in resilience, adaptability, and the indomitable human spirit.

The journey ahead, whether it leads you to the heart of dense forests, atop the craggiest peaks, or into the depths of your untapped potential, is ripe with opportunities for growth and discovery. The wilderness survival hacks we've explored are your toolkit, not just for the wilds of nature but for navigating the unpredictable terrains of everyday life.

Remember, one of the most remarkable survival hacks is how you approach challenges. It's about seeing beyond the immediate threat or discomfort and recognizing the opportunities for learning and growth that adversity presents. This mindset, cultivated in the wild, can transform obstacles into stepping stones, leading to personal growth and a deeper appreciation for the world around us.

As you prepare for your next adventure, whether a meticulously planned expedition or the spontaneous call of the wild, carry the knowledge and insights from these pages. Let them guide you in practical survival and living a life filled with adventure, learning, and a relentless pursuit of pushing beyond your limits.

In the end, the journey ahead is yours to shape. Armed with the right skills, a resilient mindset, and an open heart, there's no limit to the adventures you can embark upon. The wilderness awaits a vast, vivid classroom ready to teach its timeless lessons. Embrace it with respect, curiosity, and a readiness to learn, and you'll find that the most incredible survival hack of all is the journey itself.

WILDERNESS LIFELINE

BUSHCRAFT FIRST AID FOR ULTIMATE SURVIVAL

INTRODUCTION TO BUSHCRAFT FIRST AID

A medical kit on a bench in the wilderness.

Understanding the Basics of Bushcraft

Bushcraft, at its core, is the skill set required to thrive in the natural environment. It encompasses a broad range of

Introduction to Bushcraft First Aid

knowledge, from identifying edible plants and navigating the wilderness to creating shelters and managing fire. However, first aid is one aspect of bushcraft that is often overlooked yet equally vital. Understanding the basics of bushcraft is not just about mastering the environment; it's also about knowing how to respond to the challenges and emergencies that may arise within it.

First aid knowledge becomes indispensable in the wild for several reasons. The isolation and often remote locations mean that medical help could be away for hours if not days. In such scenarios, the ability to administer first aid can make a significant difference in the outcome of an emergency. This could range from treating minor cuts and burns to managing more severe conditions like hypothermia or heatstroke until professional help can be reached.

Moreover, the wilderness presents unique challenges and hazards not commonly encountered in urban settings. The variety of potential emergencies is vast, from insect bites and animal attacks to injuries from tools and natural elements. A solid understanding of first aid allows bushcraft enthusiasts to prepare for and respond to these specific challenges effectively. It's not just about applying a bandage; it's about knowing how to adapt and use the resources available in nature to aid in treatment. For instance, knowing which plants have antiseptic properties or how to create a splint using branches could be life-saving.

In addition to treating injuries and illnesses, first aid knowledge encompasses prevention. Understanding how to avoid common hazards, recognizing the signs of severe conditions like dehydration or frostbite, and knowing when to seek shelter can prevent emergencies from occurring in the first place. This proactive approach to health and safety is fundamental to bushcraft, ensuring that adventurers can enjoy the wilderness while minimizing risks.

First aid is a critical component of bushcraft that complements and enhances the traditional skills associated with wilderness survival. It empowers individuals to survive and do so safely, with a well-rounded understanding of how to care for themselves and others in the natural environment. As we delve deeper into the specifics of bushcraft first aid in the following sections, we will explore the practical skills and knowledge necessary to handle a wide range of situations, ensuring that enthusiasts are well-prepared for their adventures in the wild.

The Importance of First Aid Knowledge in the Wild

Venturing into the wilderness, whether for leisure or as a part of a lifestyle choice, brings with it an unparalleled sense of freedom and connection to nature. However, this adventure also exposes one to various risks and potential emergencies that can arise from the unpredictable elements of the wild. In this context, the knowledge of first aid becomes not just functional but essential. The ability to respond effectively to injuries or health issues when professional medical help is not immediately accessible can mean the difference between a minor setback and a life-threatening situation.

First aid knowledge equips you with the skills to assess and manage minor and major emergencies, from treating cuts, burns, and bites to addressing more serious concerns such as hypothermia, heatstroke, or severe allergic reactions. Understanding how to stabilize a patient until professional medical help can be reached is a critical skill set that can save lives. This is especially true in bushcraft and wilderness settings where the nearest help could be hours, if not days, away.

Moreover, being proficient in first aid instills confidence and calmness in handling emergencies, which can be contagious and help keep others calm. It also fosters a proactive approach to safety, encouraging the preparation and prevention mindset that is crucial in bushcraft. Knowing how to avoid common hazards and minimize risks through proper preparation and awareness can prevent many emergencies from occurring in the first place.

In addition to dealing with emergencies, first aid knowledge is also about maintaining one's health in the wilderness. This includes knowledge about hydration, nutrition, and the prevention of common ailments that can occur in outdoor settings. It's about making informed decisions regarding your well-being and that of your companions, ensuring that the wilderness experience remains safe and enjoyable for everyone involved.

As we delve deeper into the specifics of bushcraft first aid in the following sections, it's important to remember that this knowledge is not just about dealing with emergencies. It's also about enhancing our connection with the natural world through a deeper understanding of caring for ourselves and others in the wilderness. With this foundation, we can approach our adventures with greater confidence, respect for the wild, and a commitment to safety that ensures our experiences are enjoyable but also responsible and sustainable.

Preparing Your First Aid Kit

Having established the foundational importance of first aid knowledge in the wilderness, let's discuss preparing your first aid kit. This kit is your frontline defense against minor injuries. It could be the difference between a minor inconvenience and a major emergency. The contents of your kit should be meticulously selected to cater to the unique challenges and risks associated with bushcraft activities.

First and foremost, your kit should include a variety of bandages. This includes adhesive bandages of various sizes for minor cuts and scrapes, sterile gauze pads for larger wounds, and elastic bandages for sprains or strains. It's also wise to include a roll of medical tape to secure gauze in place.

Antiseptic wipes and antibiotic ointments are crucial for cleaning and protecting wounds from infection. The risk of infection in the wilderness is heightened due to exposure to the elements and potentially unclean conditions. Therefore, ensuring wounds are correctly cleaned and dressed is paramount.

In addition to wound care supplies, your kit should contain items to address other common ailments and injuries. This includes antihistamines for allergic reactions, pain relievers such as ibuprofen or acetaminophen, and anti-diarrheal medications. Given the nature of bushcraft activities, including a tick removal tool and insect sting relief treatment is also prudent.

A critical but often overlooked component is a pair of medical-grade gloves. These serve two essential purposes: protecting the caregiver from potential bloodborne pathogens and keeping the treatment area as sterile as possible.

A CPR mask and tourniquet can be lifesaving for more severe emergencies. While these items require proper practical training, their inclusion is recommended for those prepared to utilize them correctly.

Lastly, your first aid kit should be tailored to you and your group's specific needs and the duration and location of your trip. Consider including personal medications, a blister treatment kit for long hikes, and a thermal blanket for cold-weather environments. It's also beneficial to periodically review and update your kit, ensuring medications are within their expiry date and supplies are replenished after use.

Remember, the goal of your first aid kit is to provide the tools necessary for immediate care and offer peace of mind, allowing you to fully immerse in the bushcraft experience with the confidence that you are prepared to address minor medical needs. As we progress, we'll delve into assessing risks and planning, equipping you with the knowledge to enjoy your wilderness adventures safely.

Assessing Risks and Planning Ahead

In the realm of bushcraft, venturing into the wilderness is not without its risks. While the allure of the great outdoors beckons, it is paramount to approach each adventure with a mindset geared toward safety and preparedness. This section delves into the critical process of assessing risks and planning, ensuring you are well-equipped to handle potential emergencies in the wild.

The first step in risk assessment involves understanding the environment you plan to explore. Different terrains and climates pose unique challenges; for instance, a dense forest may harbor ticks carrying Lyme disease, while arid regions could expose you to heatstroke and dehydration. Researching the specific hazards of your destination is essential. This includes weather patterns, wildlife, and dangers like unstable terrain or toxic plants.

Once you grasp the environmental risks, it's crucial to evaluate your skill level and physical condition. Bushcraft often requires a blend of physical endurance, navigation skills, and survival knowledge. Be honest with yourself about your capabilities and limitations. If you're venturing into a particularly challenging area, consider acquiring new skills or enhancing existing ones through courses or guided practice.

Equally important is the planning phase. This encompasses route planning, informing someone of your itinerary, and estimating the duration of your trip. Always have a contingency plan if you need to alter your route due to unexpected conditions or emergencies. Technology can be a helpful ally here; GPS devices and emergency beacons can provide a safety net but do not rely on them solely. The wilderness can be unpredictable, and electronic devices may fail.

In addition to personal preparation, group dynamics should be noticed if you're not venturing alone. Ensure all members know the plan and establish clear communication and decision-making protocols. Assess the group's overall skill level and ensure that at least one member is proficient in first aid. Collective responsibility and teamwork can significantly enhance safety in bushcraft expeditions.

Lastly, part of planning ahead involves preparing for the unexpected. Despite thorough preparation, emergencies can still occur. Familiarize yourself with basic first aid procedures and carry a well-stocked kit tailored to your adventure's specific risks. Knowing how to respond to common injuries or illnesses in the wilderness can make a critical difference in the outcome of an emergency.

By meticulously assessing risks and planning, you can significantly mitigate the dangers associated with bushcraft and ensure a safer, more enjoyable experience in the wilderness. This proactive approach prepares you for potential challenges. It instills a more profound respect for the natural world and its inherent risks.

Adopting a Mindset for Survival and First Aid

The line between a minor inconvenience and a life-threatening situation can be thin in the wilderness. The ability to adapt, think clearly, and apply first aid knowledge is not just beneficial—it's essential. Adopting a mindset for survival and first aid is about mentally preparing yourself to face and overcome the challenges that nature might throw. This mindset is a blend of resilience, preparedness, and the ability to remain calm under pressure, which is crucial for effective bushcraft first aid.

Resilience is the backbone of survival. The inner strength enables you to bounce back from setbacks and continue moving forward. In bushcraft, resilience might mean enduring discomfort, like cold or hunger, without losing focus on your safety and well-being. It's about maintaining a positive attitude even when things are unplanned. Remember, your mental state can significantly influence your physical condition. A resilient mindset helps conserve energy and keep stress at bay, vital for survival.

On the other hand, preparedness is about having the knowledge and skills before you need them. It involves learning and practicing first aid techniques, understanding how to use the tools at your disposal, and being aware of the potential hazards in your

Introduction to Bushcraft First Aid

environment. Preparedness means you've equipped yourself mentally and physically for the challenges you might face. This doesn't just include packing the right gear, familiarizing yourself with the area you'll be exploring, and knowing how to respond to the injuries or health issues that could arise.

The most critical aspect of this mindset is the ability to remain calm under pressure. Panic is your greatest enemy in a survival situation. It clouds judgment, wastes energy, and can lead to poor decision-making. Cultivating calmness involves practicing stress management techniques and developing confidence in your skills and knowledge. Breathing exercises, for instance, can effectively manage stress levels and maintain clarity of thought when faced with an emergency.

To adopt this mindset:

1. Start by challenging yourself in controlled environments.
2. Practice your first aid skills regularly, not just in theory but also through practical application.
3. Engage in outdoor activities that push your comfort zone while ensuring you're never in real danger.

4. Reflect on these experiences, identifying what you did well and where you could improve.

This reflective practice builds confidence and reinforces a positive attitude towards overcoming obstacles.

In conclusion, adopting a mindset for survival and first aid in bushcraft is about more than just knowing what to do; it's about being mentally prepared. It's a combination of resilience, preparedness, and calmness under pressure. By cultivating this mindset, you equip yourself not just to survive but to thrive in the wilderness, ensuring that you can enjoy the beauty and solitude of nature with the confidence that you are prepared for whatever challenges you might face.

1
BASIC FIRST AID SKILLS

| Two adventurers performing first aid in the wilderness.

Performing CPR in the Wilderness

Performing CPR (Cardiopulmonary Resuscitation) in the wilderness requires a calm, methodical approach, especially given the potential lack of immediate professional medical assistance. This section outlines the critical steps to take when faced with a situation that necessitates CPR in a remote setting. It's imperative to remember that CPR can be life-saving when someone's breathing or heartbeat has stopped.

First, assess the situation to ensure your safety and the victim's. In the wilderness, hazards include terrain, wildlife, and the victim's condition. Once it's safe to proceed, check the victim for responsiveness by gently shaking their shoulders and asking loudly, "Are you okay?" If there is no response, call for help. If you're alone, you'll have to make a judgment call on whether to leave the victim to seek help or to start CPR immediately.

Next, check the victim's airway to ensure it is clear. Tilt the head back slightly and lift the chin to open the airway. Look, listen, and feel for breathing for no more than 10 seconds. In the absence of breathing, or if the victim is only gasping, begin CPR.

CPR in the wilderness follows the same basic principles as in more urban settings, focusing on chest compressions and rescue breaths. Place the heel of one hand on the center of the victim's chest, with your other hand on top. Interlock your fingers and ensure you're positioned directly above the victim's chest. Using your body weight, compress the chest at least 2 inches deep but not more than 2.4 inches at a rate of 100 to 120 compressions per minute. After every 30 compressions, give two rescue breaths by pinching the victim's nose shut, covering their mouth with yours, and blowing in to make the chest rise.

It's crucial to continue CPR without interruption until signs of life return, professional help arrives, or you are physically unable to continue. Help can be hours away in a wilderness setting, making your efforts vital to the victim's survival.

Remember, the effectiveness of CPR can be influenced by factors unique to the wilderness, such as extreme temperatures, which can affect both the rescuer's and the victim's physical condition. Additionally, modifications might be necessary based on the victim's age, the presence of injuries, or if the rescuer is alone without the possibility of relief.

Performing CPR is physically demanding, especially in a remote environment. If you're alone, periodically reassess the situation to determine if you need help. If you're with a group, rotate the role of rescuer to avoid exhaustion.

This guide is a basic overview, and it's strongly recommended that anyone who spends time in the wilderness undergo formal training in wilderness first aid and CPR. Such preparation can make the difference between life and death in emergencies far from immediate medical assistance.

Dealing with Bleeding and Wounds

In the wilderness, where medical help may not be immediately accessible, bushcraft enthusiasts must know how to manage bleeding and wounds effectively. This involves practical steps and techniques to control bleeding and clean and dress wounds to prevent infection and promote healing.

When faced with a bleeding wound, the primary goal is to control the bleeding as quickly as possible. This can be achieved by applying direct pressure to the wound with a clean cloth or bandage. If the bleeding is severe and does not stop with direct pressure, a pressure bandage or, in extreme cases, a tourniquet may be necessary. However, using a tourniquet should be considered a last resort due to the risk of tissue damage and should only be applied by someone trained in its use.

Once the bleeding is under control, cleaning the wound to prevent infection is next. Gently rinse away any dirt or debris with clean water. If clean water is unavailable, boiled and cooled water or a mild antiseptic solution can be used. It's important to avoid using alcohol or hydrogen peroxide directly in the wound, as these substances can damage tissue and delay healing.

After cleaning, applying a thin layer of antibiotic ointment, if available, will help prevent infection and keep the wound moist, which aids in healing. The wound should then be covered with a sterile dressing to protect it from further contamination, absorb any ongoing bleeding, and help keep it moist. The dressing should be changed daily or whenever it becomes wet or dirty. The wound should be inspected for signs of infection, such as increased redness, swelling, warmth, or pus, each time the dressing changes.

While minor wounds can often be managed effectively in the field, monitoring the wound closely for signs of infection or other complications is crucial. If the wound does not begin to heal within a few days, or if any signs of infection are noticed, medical attention should be sought as soon as possible. A healthcare professional should also evaluate wounds caused by a deep animal bite, involve a joint, or show signs of severe infection.

In summary, dealing with bleeding and wounds in the wilderness requires prompt and appropriate action to control bleeding, clean and disinfect the wound, and apply a protective dressing. Following these steps allows most minor wounds to be effectively managed and complications prevented. However, always be prepared to seek medical attention when necessary, as some wounds may require professional care to heal properly.

Managing Sprains and Fractures

In the wilderness, where medical help might be hours or even days away, knowing how to manage sprains and fractures can make a significant difference in mobility and pain management. This section covers practical steps and techniques to effectively address these common injuries, ensuring you can provide the best care in a bushcraft setting.

A sprain occurs when a ligament, the tissue connecting bones, is stretched or torn, typically in the ankles, knees, or wrists. A fracture, on the other hand, is a break in a bone. Both injuries share symptoms like pain, swelling, and limited ability to move the affected area. However, fractures may also present with visible deformity or the sound of a bone breaking at the time of injury.

Upon suspecting a sprain or fracture, the first step is to stop and assess the situation. Encourage the injured person to remain still and support the injured limb in its natural position, avoiding unnecessary movement that could exacerbate the injury.

For sprains, the **RICE** method is a widely recommended treatment plan that includes:

- **Rest** (keeping weight off the injured area)

- **Ice** (applying cold packs to reduce swelling and pain with a barrier like a cloth to prevent ice burn and limiting application to 20 minutes)
- **Compression** (wrapping the injured area with a bandage to limit swelling, ensuring it's snug but not too tight)
- **Elevation** (raising the injured limb above heart level to decrease swelling)

Fractures require immobilization to prevent further injury. If trained and safe, you can create a splint with available materials like sticks or a rolled-up magazine and secure it with bandages or cloth strips. The splint should immobilize the joints above and below the fracture site. However, if unsure about the nature of the injury or how to immobilize it adequately, it's best to leave the limb in the position found and seek professional medical help as soon as possible.

Pain management is crucial, with over-the-counter pain relievers being an option if the injured person can safely ingest them. Keeping the injured person calm and reassured can also help manage pain psychologically.

Regularly monitoring the injured person for signs of shock or worsening symptoms is essential. If the injury is severe or there's no improvement, evacuation to a medical facility becomes necessary. In a bushcraft context, this might mean self-evacuation or activating emergency response systems if available.

In conclusion, managing sprains and fractures in the wilderness requires a calm and methodical approach. By understanding these basic first aid techniques, you can provide essential care to reduce pain and prevent further injury until professional medical help can be reached. Prevention is the best treatment, so always take necessary precautions to avoid injuries when engaging in bushcraft activities.

Recognizing and Treating Hypothermia and Heatstroke

Understanding how to recognize and treat hypothermia and heatstroke is crucial in the wilderness, where the elements can be as much a foe as any other hazard. These conditions represent the body's inability to regulate its temperature, either dropping too low (hypothermia) or rising too high (heatstroke). Both can be life-threatening if not addressed promptly and adequately.

Recognizing and Treating Hypothermia

Hypothermia occurs when the body loses heat faster than it can produce it, causing the core body temperature to fall below 95°F (35°C). It can happen in any environment, not just those covered in snow or ice. Wind, rain, and immersion in cold water can all lead to hypothermia.

Symptoms include shivering (which may cease as hypothermia worsens), confusion, slurred speech, drowsiness, and, in severe cases, loss of consciousness. The person may also exhibit paradoxical undressing, where they begin to remove clothing due to feeling hot when they are cold.

Treatment begins with moving the person to a sheltered environment to protect them from the cold. Remove any wet clothing and replace it with dry, warm layers. Insulate them from the cold ground using sleeping pads or layers of clothing. Warm, sweet beverages can help increase the body's temperature, but avoid alcohol or caffeine. Gentle rewarming is critical; too rapid heating can be dangerous. If available, use warm (not hot) water bottles or heat packs placed in the armpits, groin, and along the sides of the chest. Monitor the person's breathing and be prepared to perform CPR if they become unresponsive.

Recognizing and Treating Heatstroke

Conversely, heatstroke occurs when the body overheats, typically due to prolonged exposure to or physical exertion in high temperatures. The body's temperature regulation system becomes overwhelmed, leading to a core body temperature of 104°F (40°C) or higher.

Symptoms include confusion, altered mental state, slurred speech, nausea, vomiting, rapid breathing, flushed skin, and, in severe cases, loss of consciousness. Unlike heat exhaustion, a precursor to heatstroke, the person may stop sweating.

Treatment focuses on rapidly lowering the body's temperature. Move the person to a shaded or air-conditioned area. Remove excess clothing to increase heat loss. Apply wet cloths to the skin, or immerse the person in cool (not cold) water if possible—fan air over the person while wetting their skin to increase cooling through evaporation. Offer sips of water if the person is conscious and can drink, but do not force fluids. Monitor their condition closely and seek emergency medical help immediately. Heatstroke is a severe condition that requires professional medical treatment.

In both hypothermia and heatstroke, prevention is critical. Dress appropriately for the environment, stay hydrated, and avoid extreme temperature exposures when possible. Understanding these conditions and their treatments empowers you to act decisively, potentially saving lives in the wilderness.

Creating and Using Splints from Natural Materials

In the wilderness, the ability to improvise with available resources can be a lifesaver, especially when it comes to administering first aid. One common scenario where bushcraft skills come into play is in creating and applying splints using natural materials. This guide will help you identify suitable materials and construct effective splints for different injuries.

The first step in creating a natural splint is finding sturdy yet somewhat flexible materials to support and immobilize the injured limb. Ideal materials include straight, strong branches free of rot or excessive flexibility. They should be longer than the injured area to ensure proper support. Large pieces, like birch bark, are also suitable due to their flexibility and strength. Additionally, flexible vines or roots can keep the splint in place but ensure they are strong enough to hold it without breaking.

Once you have gathered your materials, you should prepare the limb by ensuring the injured area is as comfortable and aligned as possible, avoiding excessive movement, especially if a fracture is suspected. If possible, pad the injured area with soft materials such as moss, leaves, or clothing to prevent pressure sores and discomfort. Then, place the rigid materials (sticks, branches, or bark) along the injured limb's sides, ensuring they extend beyond the joints above and below the injury. A single splint along the injured digit may suffice for fingers or toes.

Securing the splint involves using vines, roots, strips of fabric, or even shoelaces to tie the splint in place. Start by securing the splint above and below the injury site, avoiding tying directly over the injury. The ties should be firm to immobilize the limb but not so tight as to cut off circulation. You can check for adequate blood flow by pressing on a fingernail or toenail; the color should return within a few seconds.

After applying the splint, monitoring the injured person for signs of decreased circulation, such as increased pain, swelling, or a bluish tint to the skin, is essential. Adjust the splint as necessary to ensure comfort and safety. While creating and applying a splint from natural materials can be crucial in a wilderness emergency, it is temporary. Always seek professional medical help as soon as possible. Suppose you need clarification about the severity of the injury or how to apply a splint properly. In that case, it's better to immobilize the limb with soft padding and seek help rather than risk further injury by misapplying a splint.

In conclusion, creating and using splints from natural materials is a valuable skill in bushcraft first aid. By following these guidelines, you can provide essential support to an injured limb and prevent further damage while awaiting professional medical care. Remember, the key to adequate first aid is a calm and methodical approach, ensuring the safety and comfort of the injured person throughout the process.

Chapter Summary

- Performing CPR in the wilderness requires a calm approach and immediate action, focusing on chest compressions and rescue breaths.
- Ensure personal and victim safety before proceeding with CPR, checking for responsiveness and breathing before starting compressions.
- Continue CPR without interruption until professional help arrives or the victim shows signs of life.
- Wilderness conditions, such as extreme temperatures, may affect CPR effectiveness and require modifications based on the victim's condition.
- Managing bleeding involves applying direct pressure, cleaning and disinfecting the wound, and using a sterile dressing to promote healing.

- Sprains and fractures should be managed using the RICE method for sprains and immobilization for fractures, with pain management and monitoring for complications.
- Recognizing and treating hypothermia and heatstroke are crucial in wilderness settings, focusing on rewarming or cooling the victim, respectively.
- Creating splints from natural materials involves finding sturdy supports, securing them to immobilize the injured limb, and monitoring circulation issues.

2

NATURAL REMEDIES AND PLANT MEDICINE

An array of medicinal plants and herbs on a workbench.

Identifying Medicinal Plants

In the wilderness, identifying medicinal plants is crucial for emergency first aid and long-term survival skills.

This knowledge allows for the treatment of various ailments with natural remedies. It fosters a deep connection with the natural environment. The process involves recognizing and utilizing medicinal plants, focusing on their identification, harvesting, and the ethical considerations involved.

The initial step in using plant medicine is to identify the plants accurately. This requires observation skills and sometimes a bit of study. Start by familiarizing yourself with a few common plants in your area, learning about their characteristics, habitats, and any similar-looking plants that could be harmful. Using field guides specific to your region, which provide detailed descriptions and photographs, can be extremely helpful.

Additionally, joining a local foraging group or workshop can offer hands-on experience with the guidance of experts.

When identifying plants, it's essential to examine their leaves, flowers, stems, and roots closely, noting their shape, color, and distinctive features. Some plants may only be identifiable when they bloom, while others can be recognized by their foliage or bark. Understanding botanical terminology can significantly improve your identification skills, making understanding and sharing your findings more accessible.

After positively identifying a plant as medicinal and safe, the next step is to harvest it responsibly. This means taking only what you need and ensuring the plant can continue to thrive. Use clean, sharp tools for precise cuts, aiding the plant's recovery. The timing of harvesting is also vital to preserving the plant's medicinal properties; for example, leaves and flowers are best collected in the morning when their essential oils are most concentrated. At the same time, roots are typically harvested in the fall.

Ethical foraging is essential when collecting medicinal plants. This includes getting permission to forage on private land, respecting protected areas, and avoiding endangered species. Sustainable foraging practices are crucial, such as taking only what you need and leaving no trace. It's also important to consider the ecological impact of removing plants from their habitat and harvesting in a way that allows plant populations to regenerate.

In summary, identifying and harvesting medicinal plants are critical skills in bushcraft first aid, offering a way to harness nature's healing power. By practicing these skills with respect, care, and a willingness to learn, you can use plant medicine safely and sustainably to support health and well-being in the wilderness. The following steps involve transforming these raw materials into effective poultices and salves, further enhancing your bushcraft first aid capabilities.

Preparing Poultices and Salves

In bushcraft first aid, preparing poultices and salves from natural resources can be a vital skill for treating various injuries and ailments when conventional medical supplies are unavailable. This section delves into the practical aspects of creating these remedies using medicinal plants identified in the wild.

A poultice is a soft, moist mass of plant material applied directly to the skin to relieve soreness and inflammation. It can treat insect bites, stings, cuts, bruises, and infections. To prepare a poultice, follow these steps:

1. **Select the appropriate plant:** Based on the ailment, choose a plant known for its medicinal properties. For example, plantain leaves (Plantago major) are excellent for cuts and insect bites due to their anti-inflammatory and antiseptic properties.
2. **Crush or grind the plant material:** Use a mortar and pestle, a stone, or simply your hands to crush the leaves, roots, or flowers of the plant to release its medicinal compounds. Adding a small amount of water can help if the plant is too dry.

3. **Apply to the affected area:** Spread the crushed plant material directly onto the skin over the affected area. If the injury is open, ensure the plant material is clean and free from contaminants.
4. **Secure the poultice:** Use a clean cloth or bandage to hold the poultice in place. It's essential to keep the poultice moist for its active components to be effective.
5. **Duration:** Leave the poultice on for up to 4 hours. Monitor the skin for adverse reactions, such as increased irritation or allergies.

Salves, or ointments, are thickened preparations to heal and protect the skin. They are handy for treating dry skin, chapped lips, burns, and wounds. To make an essential herbal salve:

1. **Infuse oils with medicinal plants:** Begin by infusing a carrier oil (such as coconut oil, olive oil, or almond oil) with your chosen medicinal plant. This can be done by gently heating the oil and plant material in a double boiler for 2-3 hours, ensuring the oil does not overheat.
2. **Strain the plant material:** After the infusion process, strain the oil through a fine mesh

strainer or cheesecloth to remove the plant material, leaving behind the infused oil.
3. **Thicken the salve:** Add beeswax to the infused oil. A general guideline is to use approximately 1 ounce (28 grams) of beeswax per cup (240 ml) of infused oil. Gently heat the mixture until the beeswax melts completely.
4. **Cool and solidify:** Pour the mixture into clean containers and allow it to cool and solidify. Adding essential oils for additional therapeutic benefits can be done at this stage, ensuring they are thoroughly mixed before the salve hardens.
5. **Storage:** Store the salve in a cool, dark place. Properly made salves can last for up to a year.

By mastering the preparation of poultices and salves, one can effectively utilize the healing power of nature. These traditional remedies, derived from the knowledge of identifying medicinal plants, offer a sustainable and accessible form of first aid in the wilderness. As we progress, understanding the role of natural antiseptics will further enhance our ability to manage injuries and infections in a bushcraft setting.

Natural Antiseptics in the Wild

Nature offers its pharmacy in the wilderness, where conventional medical supplies might not be readily available. Understanding how to harness the natural antiseptics found in the wild can be a crucial skill for anyone practicing bushcraft or simply spending time in nature. This section delves into identifying and using natural antiseptics to prevent infection and promote healing in cuts, scrapes, and other wounds.

One of the most readily available natural antiseptics is honey. Known for its antibacterial properties, honey can be applied directly to wounds to prevent infection and promote healing. Its high viscosity helps to create a protective barrier over the wound, keeping it clean and moist, which is conducive to healing. When sourcing honey in the wild, ensure it is from a clean and uncontaminated source.

Another powerful natural antiseptic is garlic. Garlic contains allicin, a compound with significant antibacterial and antifungal properties. Crushing fresh garlic cloves and applying them to wounds can help prevent infection. However, due to its potency, it's advisable to use garlic cautiously as it can cause skin irritation in some individuals.

The sap of certain trees, such as pine or birch, also serves as an effective natural antiseptic. These saps contain compounds that inhibit the growth of bacteria and fungi. To use, apply a small amount of sap directly to the wound. The sap not only helps prevent infection but can also act as a natural bandage, sealing the wound from external contaminants.

Aloe vera is another valuable natural antiseptic widely recognized for its soothing and healing properties. The gel inside the aloe vera leaves can be applied to wounds to reduce inflammation and fight bacteria. Its cooling effect relieves pain and itching associated with minor wounds and burns.

Lastly, the plantain leaf, commonly found in many parts of the world, is an effective wound remedy. The leaves contain antibacterial and anti-inflammatory properties. Crushed or chewed plantain leaves can be applied directly to the wound or as a poultice. This not only helps prevent infection but also soothes the affected area.

Incorporating these natural antiseptics into your bushcraft first aid kit can significantly enhance your ability to manage wounds effectively in the wild. It's important to remember that while these natural remedies can be beneficial, they are not substitutes for professional medical treatment in serious cases. Always seek medical attention for severe wounds or if there's a risk of infection that doesn't improve with basic first aid measures.

Using Herbs for Pain Relief

Understanding the natural resources available for managing pain is vital in bushcraft and wilderness survival. This section delves into the practical use of herbs for pain relief, a cornerstone of natural remedies and plant medicine. It's important to note that while these methods can provide relief, they should not replace professional medical treatment when it's available. However, these natural solutions can be invaluable in situations where conventional medicine is not an option.

Willow bark, often referred to as nature's aspirin, contains salicin, a chemical similar to the active ingredient in aspirin. Various cultures have harnessed willow bark's properties for centuries to alleviate pain and reduce fever. To use willow bark for pain relief, one can chew on the bark directly or brew a tea. To prepare the tea, simmer about two teaspoons of shredded bark in a cup of water for 10 to 15 minutes, then let it steep for an additional half hour. Drinking this tea can help ease pain from headaches, lower back discomfort, and arthritis. Use of willow bark judiciously is crucial, as excessive consumption can lead to stomach irritation or more severe health issues.

Turmeric is a powerful anti-inflammatory herb that can treat many pains and aches, especially inflammation-related. The active component in turmeric, curcumin, is responsible for its pain-relieving effects. Incorporating turmeric into your diet or applying a paste made from turmeric powder and water to the affected area can help reduce inflammation and alleviate pain. For internal use, adding a teaspoon of turmeric to a warm drink or meal daily can offer systemic pain relief.

Lavender is renowned for its calming and soothing properties, making it an excellent herb for relieving stress and tension headaches. The aroma of lavender alone can act as a mild sedative, helping to reduce pain perception. For topical application, lavender oil can be diluted with carrier oil and massaged into the temples or the back of the neck to alleviate headache pain. Additionally, inhaling lavender essential oil or using it in a diffuser can help create a relaxing environment conducive to pain relief.

Peppermint is another herb with significant pain-relieving properties, particularly for digestive discomfort and headaches. The menthol in peppermint acts as a natural analgesic, providing a cooling sensation that can soothe pain. For headaches, applying diluted peppermint oil to the forehead has been shown to reduce the intensity and duration of pain. Peppermint tea is an effective remedy to alleviate digestive issues. Steep a teaspoon of dried peppermint leaves in boiling water for 10 minutes, strain, and drink.

Ginger, with its potent anti-inflammatory and

analgesic properties, is effective in treating a variety of pains, including menstrual cramps and joint pain. Ginger can be consumed fresh, dried, as a tea, or applied topically. For pain relief, drinking ginger tea is particularly beneficial. To make ginger tea, simmer a piece of fresh ginger root in water for 15 to 20 minutes, then strain and enjoy. Ginger's warmth not only alleviates pain but also helps improve circulation, which can speed up the healing process.

Incorporating these herbs into your bushcraft first aid kit can provide natural, effective options for managing pain in the wilderness. Remember, the key to using any natural remedy is knowledge and moderation. Understanding the correct preparation and dosage is crucial to ensuring these remedies are safe and effective. As we transition from discussing natural pain relief methods, it's essential to consider the broader context of health and healing in the wilderness, including the role of nutrition in supporting the body's recovery processes.

The Role of Nutrition in Healing

In the wilderness, where conventional medical resources are scarce, the importance of nutrition in healing cannot be overstated. The body's ability to repair itself, fight infections, and recover from injuries is significantly enhanced by the nutrients we consume. This section delves into the role of nutrition in healing, focusing on how certain foods and natural resources found in the wild can bolster our health and aid in recovery.

First and foremost, it's essential to understand that a balanced diet is critical in maintaining overall health and optimizing the body's healing processes. Essential nutrients such as proteins, vitamins, minerals, and antioxidants contribute to tissue repair, immune function, and the reduction of inflammation.

Proteins are the building blocks of the body, essential for the repair of tissues and creating new cells. In a bushcraft scenario, protein sources might include fish, wild game, insects, and certain plants and nuts. Consuming adequate amounts of protein can significantly speed up the healing process of wounds and injuries.

Vitamins and minerals, particularly vitamins A, C, D, and E, along with zinc, iron, and selenium, play pivotal roles in healing and immune function. Vitamin C, found in wild berries and certain greens, produces collagen. This protein helps heal wounds by repairing damaged skin and tissues. Vitamin A, sourced from leafy green vegetables and some animal products, supports cell growth and boosts the immune system. Meanwhile, vitamin D, obtained from sunlight exposure, aids in calcium absorption and bone healing.

Antioxidants in various wild plants and fruits combat

oxidative stress and reduce inflammation, which is vital in the healing process. Foods rich in antioxidants include berries, nuts, and herbs that can be foraged in the wild.

Hydration is another critical aspect of nutrition in healing. Water is essential for all bodily functions, including transporting nutrients to cells and removing toxins from the body. Ensuring adequate hydration is a simple yet effective way to support the body's natural healing processes.

Incorporating wild edibles into your diet can provide these essential nutrients when conventional food sources are unavailable. Foraging for wild plants, however, requires knowledge of safe and nutritious options specific to the area. Some common edible plants include dandelions, which are rich in vitamins A and C, and nettles, a good source of protein, vitamins, and minerals.

Understanding the nutritional value of available resources and how they can support the body's healing processes is a valuable skill in bushcraft first aid. By prioritizing nutrition and making informed choices about the foods we consume in the wilderness, we can enhance our resilience, accelerate healing, and maintain optimal health in challenging environments.

Chapter Summary

- Medicinal plants are essential for emergency first aid and survival in the wilderness, offering natural treatment options and a deeper environmental connection.
- Identifying medicinal plants accurately requires knowledge of their features, habitats, and similar species, with field guides and local groups as critical resources.
- Harvest medicinal plants respectfully and sustainably, using clean tools and ensuring plants can regrow. Depending on the plant part needed, specific harvesting times are required.
- Ethical foraging involves getting permission, respecting protected areas, avoiding endangered species, and practicing sustainability to allow plant regeneration.
- Preparing poultices and salves includes selecting the appropriate plant, crushing or grinding it, applying it directly, or infusing it in oils with beeswax for salves.
- In a natural first aid kit, natural antiseptics like honey, garlic, tree sap, aloe vera, and

plantain leaf are crucial for preventing infection and aiding wound healing.

- Herbs such as willow bark, turmeric, lavender, peppermint, and ginger offer natural pain relief through teas, pastes, and infused oils.

- Nutrition, including proteins, vitamins, minerals, antioxidants, and hydration, is vital for healing, immune function, and health. It emphasizes the importance of a balanced diet and foraging for wild edibles.

3

HANDLING ANIMAL AND INSECT BITES

A first aid kit in the wilderness.

Identifying Dangerous Animals and Insects

In the wilderness, identifying potentially dangerous animals and insects is crucial for ensuring your safety and well-being. This knowledge helps avoid unwanted encounters and prepares you for the appropriate response in case of a bite or sting. The variety of fauna that one might encounter is vast. Still, specific characteristics and behaviors can help in recognizing the threats.

Starting with snakes, many species are harmless, but it's the venomous ones that bushcraft enthusiasts need to be wary of. Venomous snakes can often be identified by their distinctive head shapes, which are usually broader and more triangular than non-venomous snakes due to their venom glands. Additionally, in some regions, elliptical pupils can indicate venomous species. However, these characteristics are not universal, and learning about the specific snake species in your activity area is highly recommended.

Spiders are another group of concern. While the vast majority are harmless, there are a few species, such as the Black Widow and the Brown Recluse, whose bites can cause serious health issues. These spiders tend to be reclusive and only bite when threatened. Recognizing their distinctive markings and preferred habitats can prevent unwanted encounters. For instance, the Black Widow is known for its shiny black color and the red hourglass shape on its underside.

Insects, including bees, wasps, and hornets, can also pose risks, especially to individuals with allergies to their stings. These insects are generally more aggressive when their nests are disturbed. Recognizing nest sites and understanding these insects' behavior can help avoid them. For example, wasps and hornets can be more aggressive and are likely to attack in swarms if their nests, often found hanging from trees or under eaves, are disturbed.

Ticks, though small, are significant carriers of diseases such as Lyme disease. They are often found in wooded or grassy areas and can attach to the skin of humans and animals. Checking for ticks and knowing how to remove them safely is crucial after spending time in their habitats.

Understanding these animals' and insects' behavior and habitat is critical to avoiding dangerous encounters. For instance, many venomous snakes are more active at night, and avoiding their habitats during these times can reduce the risk of encounters. Similarly, wearing protective clothing and being vigilant in areas known to harbor ticks can prevent bites.

In conclusion, the ability to identify potentially dangerous animals and insects is an essential component of bushcraft first aid. It enables individuals to take preventive measures and apply the correct first aid procedures in case of an encounter. Knowledge of the local fauna and an understanding of their behavior and habitats is invaluable for anyone venturing into the wilderness.

First Aid for Snake Bites

In the wilderness, encountering a snake and, worse, suffering a bite can be a harrowing experience. However, the situation can be managed effectively with the proper knowledge and actions. This section delves into the first aid measures that should be taken if someone is bitten by a snake, focusing on practical and immediate steps to mitigate the effects of the bite and ensure the victim's safety until professional medical help can be reached.

First and foremost, it's crucial to remain calm. Panic can accelerate the heart rate, potentially causing the venom to spread more quickly through the body. Keep the victim as still as possible, reassuring them that help is coming. Identifying the snake can be helpful for treatment, but it should not jeopardize anyone's safety. If possible, take note of the snake's appearance from a safe distance.

The next step is immobilizing the bitten limb, but avoid applying a tourniquet or cutting into the wound. These outdated methods can cause more harm than good. Instead, gently wash the bite area with soap and water, if available, to remove any venom on the skin surface. Cover the bite with a clean, dry dressing to protect it from infection.

It's imperative to keep the bitten limb immobilized and as still as possible, ideally at or slightly below heart level. This helps to slow the spread of venom. Construct a splint, if necessary, using whatever materials are at hand to prevent movement of the affected area.

Do not administer any medications, including painkillers or anti-inflammatory drugs, unless advised by a medical professional. Also, refrain from giving the victim anything to eat or drink, especially alcohol or caffeine, as these substances could exacerbate the body's reaction to the venom.

Seeking medical assistance immediately is the most critical step. If in a remote location, send someone for help or use a communication device to call emergency services. Provide them with as much information as possible about the situation, including the type of snake, if known, the time of the bite, and the victim's current condition.

While waiting for help to arrive, monitor the victim closely for any signs of shock or changes in their condition. Keep them warm, comfortable, and still. Reassure them that help is on the way and that staying calm is essential for their recovery.

In summary, the key to handling snake bites effectively is to remain calm, immobilize and protect the bite area, avoid harmful interventions, and seek professional medical help immediately. By following these steps, you can provide essential first aid that could make a significant difference in the outcome for the victim.

Treating Insect Stings and Bites

In the wilderness, insect stings and bites are not only shared. Still, they can also pose significant risks if not treated properly. This section provides a comprehensive guide to managing these incidents, ensuring safety and minimizing discomfort.

When dealing with insect stings, the first step is to remain calm. Panic can accelerate the spread of venom in the body. It should be removed if the stinger is still present, as is often the case with bee stings. However, care must be taken to scrape it out sideways with a fingernail or a blunt object like a credit card rather than tweezers, which can squeeze more venom into the skin.

Once the stinger is removed, wash the area with soap and water to prevent infection. Applying cold compresses or ice packs can help reduce swelling and pain. It's crucial to monitor for signs of an allergic reaction, including difficulty breathing, swelling of the face or mouth, or a rash spreading away from the bite site. In such cases, immediate medical attention is necessary.

For bites from insects such as mosquitoes, flies, and ants, the emphasis should be on alleviating itching and discomfort while preventing infection. After washing the affected area, applying a soothing lotion or cream containing hydrocortisone or calamine can provide relief. An oral antihistamine may also help reduce itching and swelling. To avoid infection, refrain from scratching the bite. If signs of infection such as increased redness, swelling, or pus develop, seek medical attention.

In cases of multiple stings or bites, or if the victim is known to have severe allergic reactions, it's imperative to seek medical help immediately. Carrying an epinephrine auto-injector (EpiPen) and antihistamines can be life-saving for individuals with known severe allergies.

Preventive measures are also a key component of managing insect stings and bites. Wearing protective clothing, using insect repellent, and avoiding scented products can significantly reduce the risk of being bitten or stung. Additionally, being aware of one's surroundings and avoiding areas known for high insect activity, such as stagnant water or dense woods, can minimize encounters with potentially harmful insects.

Following these guidelines, individuals can effectively manage insect stings and bites, ensuring a safer and more enjoyable wilderness experience.

Preventing and Treating Tick Bites

In the wilderness, ticks are not merely a nuisance; they are carriers of Lyme disease, Rocky Mountain spotted fever, and several other tick-borne illnesses. Understanding how to prevent tick bites and properly remove a tick is crucial for anyone venturing into tick-prone areas.

Preventing tick bites begins with the proper clothing and gear. Wear long sleeves and long pants when moving through areas known for ticks, such as wooded or grassy areas. Tuck your pants into your socks to create a barrier against ticks climbing up your legs. Light-colored clothing can make it easier to spot ticks before they find their way to your skin.

Applying insect repellent that contains 20% or more DEET, picaridin, or IR3535 on exposed skin and clothing can significantly reduce the risk of tick bites. Treat clothing and gear, such as boots, pants, and tents, with products containing 0.5% permethrin for added protection. It's essential to follow the product instructions for proper application and reapplication.

After spending time in tick-infested areas, conduct a thorough tick check on yourself, your children, and your pets. Pay close attention to under the arms, in and around the ears, inside the belly button, behind the knees, between the legs, around the waist, and especially in the hair. Showering within two hours of coming indoors can help wash off unattached ticks and provide an excellent opportunity to conduct a tick check.

If you find a tick attached to your skin, removing it as soon as possible is essential. The longer a tick is attached, the greater the risk of disease transmission. Use fine-tipped tweezers to grasp the tick as close to the skin's surface as possible. Pull upward with steady, even pressure. Do not twist or jerk the tick, which can cause the mouth parts to break off and remain in the skin. If this happens, attempt to remove the mouth parts with the tweezers. If unable to remove the mouth entirely, leave it alone and let the skin heal.

After removing the tick, thoroughly clean the bite area and your hands with rubbing alcohol, an iodine scrub, or soap and water. Dispose of a live tick by submerging it in alcohol, placing it in a sealed bag/container, wrapping it tightly in tape, or flushing it down the toilet. Never crush a tick with your fingers.

Monitor the bite site for several weeks for signs of tick-borne illness, such as rash or fever. If you develop symptoms, consult a healthcare provider promptly. Be sure to tell them about the recent tick bite, when it occurred, and where you most likely acquired it.

Understanding and implementing these preventive measures and tick removal techniques can significantly reduce the risks associated with tick bites. The following section will delve into the prevention and first response to another critical concern in the wilderness: rabies.

Rabies Prevention and First Response

The risk of encountering animals that may carry rabies is a genuine concern for bushcraft enthusiasts in the wilderness. Rabies is a fatal viral disease affecting mammals' central nervous system, including humans. It is transmitted through the saliva of infected animals, typically through bites. This section provides a comprehensive guide on rabies prevention and the first response to potential rabies exposure in a bushcraft setting.

Preventing rabies starts with understanding and avoiding unnecessary risks. Here are essential preventive measures:

1. **Vaccination:** If you're planning extended stays in areas known for rabies, consider getting vaccinated before your trip. Rabies pre-exposure vaccination involves a series of injections that provide protection but do not eliminate the need for additional treatment if bitten.
2. **Wildlife Awareness:** Educate yourself about the wildlife in the area you'll be exploring.

Avoid attracting or approaching wild animals, especially if they appear sick or behave unusually.
3. **Secure Food and Trash:** Animals, including potential rabies carriers like raccoons, bats, and foxes, are attracted to food. Store your food securely and manage your trash to avoid attracting them to your campsite.
4. **Pet Protection:** If your bushcraft adventure includes pets, ensure they are vaccinated against rabies. Keep pets on a leash and under close supervision.

Swift action is crucial if an animal bites you or someone in your group. Here's what to do:

1. **Immediate Care:** Wash the wound thoroughly with soap and water for at least 15 minutes. This can significantly reduce the viral load.
2. **Stop the Bleeding:** Apply gentle pressure with a clean cloth to stop bleeding.
3. **Disinfect:** After washing, apply an antiseptic solution to the wound to minimize infection risk.
4. **Seek Medical Attention:** Even if the wound seems minor, seeking a professional medical

evaluation as soon as possible is essential. Inform the healthcare provider about the bite and your concerns about rabies.

5. **Observe the Animal:** If it's safe, observe the animal from a distance. Information about its behavior and appearance can be crucial for healthcare providers. However, do not attempt to capture or kill the animal yourself.
6. **Follow-Up:** Post-exposure prophylaxis (PEP) injections may be necessary if rabies exposure is suspected. The treatment is highly effective if started promptly.

Remember, while the wilderness offers remarkable experiences, it poses unique challenges. Rabies prevention and how to respond to animal bites are critical components of bushcraft first aid. By taking preventive measures and being prepared to act quickly in case of an animal bite, you can enjoy your bushcraft adventures with greater peace of mind.

Chapter Summary

- Recognize dangerous animals and insects (e.g., venomous snakes, Black Widow, Brown Recluse) for safety.

- Understand the aggressive behaviors of bees, wasps, hornets, and disease risks from ticks.
- Treat snake bites by remaining calm, immobilizing the limb, washing the area, and seeking immediate medical help.
- Handle insect stings by removing the stinger carefully, washing the area, applying cold compresses, and watching for allergies.
- Prevent tick bites with protective clothing, insect repellent, thorough checks, and prompt tick removal.
- Avoid rabies by getting vaccinated, avoiding wild animals, securing food/trash, and ensuring pet vaccinations.
- Immediate, correct response to bites or stings includes washing, disinfecting, immobilizing the area, and getting medical advice.
- Knowledge of local wildlife, behaviors, habitats, and preventive measures, such as appropriate clothing and repellents, is crucial for wilderness safety.

4
WATER SAFETY AND HYDRATION

| An adventurer purifying water in the wilderness.

Finding and Purifying Water

Finding and purifying water is a critical skill for survival in the wilderness. Still, recognizing when your body needs hydration is equally important. Dehydration can occur more quickly than many realize, especially in hot, dry, or high-altitude environments. Understanding the signs of dehydration is essential for anyone venturing into the outdoors, as it can prevent serious health issues and ensure a safe return from your adventures.

The initial signs of dehydration are often subtle and easily overlooked, especially during activities that demand your focus. Thirst is the most obvious indicator, yet you're already dehydrated by the time you feel thirsty. This is why drinking water at regular intervals, especially during physical exertion, is crucial rather than waiting to feel thirsty.

Other early signs include dry mouth, fatigue, and decreased urine output. Urine color is a valuable indicator of hydration levels; light, straw-colored urine typically signifies adequate hydration, whereas dark yellow or amber-colored urine is a clear sign of dehydration. Monitoring these signs closely is essential, as they can quickly escalate to more severe symptoms if not addressed.

As dehydration progresses, symptoms become more pronounced, including headache, dizziness, or lightheadedness, particularly when standing up. These symptoms are often accompanied by dry skin, decreased sweat production, and muscle cramps. In severe cases, dehydration can lead to confusion, rapid heartbeat, rapid breathing, and even fainting. If any of these severe symptoms occur, seeking medical attention immediately is imperative.

To prevent dehydration, start by ensuring you're well-hydrated before embarking on any outdoor activities. Carry sufficient water supplies and plan for ways to replenish your water if you will be out for extended periods. Remember, in hot or humid conditions or at high altitudes, your body will require more water than usual. Additionally, incorporating electrolyte-replenishing drinks or snacks can help maintain the balance of fluids and electrolytes in your body, especially during prolonged exertion.

In summary, recognizing the signs of dehydration is a fundamental aspect of bushcraft first aid. By staying vigilant and proactive about hydration, you can prevent dehydration and its potentially dangerous consequences, ensuring a safer and more enjoyable wilderness experience.

Recognizing Signs of Dehydration

In the wilderness, where resources can be scarce, and conditions are harsh, maintaining proper hydration is not just a matter of comfort but of survival. Dehydration can set in quickly, especially during the strenuous activities often associated with bushcraft, such as hiking, building shelters, or even finding and purifying water itself. Recognizing the signs of dehydration early is crucial to prevent a manageable situation from escalating into a life-threatening emergency.

Dehydration occurs when your body loses more fluids than it takes in, leading to an imbalance that affects its normal functions. The initial symptoms can be subtle and easily overlooked, especially when your focus is on the tasks at hand. Surprisingly, thirst is not the most reliable indicator, as you may already be dehydrated by the time you feel thirsty. Instead, look for other early signs, such as a dry or sticky mouth, fatigue, and decreased urine output. The color of your urine is a valuable indicator of your hydration status; a pale straw color suggests adequate hydration, while darker shades indicate dehydration.

As dehydration progresses, the symptoms become more pronounced and harder to ignore. You may experience dizziness, confusion, or irritability, impairing your judgment and physical performance. Severe dehydration can lead to more alarming signs, including a rapid but weak pulse, low blood pressure, and sunken eyes. In extreme cases, delirium or unconsciousness can occur, signaling a medical emergency that requires immediate attention.

It's important to understand that dehydration can exacerbate the effects of other illnesses and conditions, making it harder for the body to cope with infections or recover from injuries. Furthermore, preventing dehydration becomes even more critical in a bushcraft setting, where medical help may not be readily available.

To combat dehydration, start by ensuring you consume adequate water regularly, even if you do not feel thirsty. Pay attention to the color of your urine as a gauge for your hydration levels, and adjust your fluid intake accordingly. In environments where sweating is likely, such as during physical exertion or in hot climates, increase your water intake to compensate for the loss of fluids through sweat. Additionally, be mindful of the signs of dehydration in yourself and others, especially in a group. Early detection and prompt action can prevent dehydration from becoming a severe threat to your health and safety in the wilderness.

In conclusion, recognizing the signs of dehydration is a fundamental skill in bushcraft first aid. By staying informed and vigilant, you can ensure that you and your companions remain hydrated and healthy, ready to face the challenges and enjoy the rewards of the great outdoors.

Treating Waterborne Illnesses

In the wilderness, water is both a life-sustaining resource and a potential source of illness. When hydration becomes a matter of concern, it's crucial to understand how to find and purify water and treat waterborne illnesses that might arise despite precautions. This section delves into the practical steps and knowledge required to manage such conditions, ensuring your bushcraft adventures remain safe and enjoyable.

In untreated water sources, waterborne illnesses are primarily caused by pathogens such as bacteria, viruses, and protozoa. Symptoms can range from mild gastrointestinal discomfort to severe dehydration and, in extreme cases, life-threatening conditions. Recognizing the signs of these illnesses early on is critical to effective treatment and recovery.

The first step in treating waterborne illnesses is to ensure the affected individual remains hydrated. Dehydration can exacerbate symptoms and lead to more severe health issues. Begin by providing small, frequent sips of clean, purified water. Avoid giving large amounts of water at once, as this can overwhelm the digestive system of someone already ill.

Oral rehydration solutions (ORS) are particularly effective in preventing dehydration caused by diarrhea and vomiting, common symptoms of waterborne diseases. These solutions, which can be pre-packaged or made by mixing six teaspoons of sugar and half a teaspoon of salt in 1 liter of purified water, help replenish lost fluids and electrolytes. It's advisable to have ORS packets as part of your first aid kit when venturing into the wilderness.

In cases where symptoms persist or worsen, seeking medical attention is crucial. Some waterborne illnesses may require antibiotics or specific treatments that can only be prescribed by a healthcare professional; however, in remote areas where immediate medical help is unavailable, knowing how to recognize and manage the initial symptoms can be life-saving.

Preventive measures are equally important to prevent waterborne illnesses. Always purify water by boiling, filtering, or using chemical treatments before drinking or using it for cooking. Be mindful of your water sources, avoiding those likely to be contaminated by human or animal waste.

Understanding the risks and symptoms of waterborne illnesses and knowing how to treat and prevent them is essential for anyone venturing into the wilderness. You can enjoy the natural world with confidence and security by ensuring access to clean, safe water and being prepared to address any health issues that arise.

Safe Swimming Practices

Water is both a vital resource and a potential hazard in the wilderness. While we've discussed the importance of treating water to prevent illness, addressing the risks associated with swimming in natural water bodies is equally crucial. Safe swimming practices in the wilderness are about personal safety, preserving one's health, and ensuring that water sources remain uncontaminated and safe for consumption.

First and foremost, always assess the water conditions before deciding to swim. Look for signs of pollution or contamination, such as floating debris, oil slicks, or unusual colors and odors. Remember, water safe for swimming is only necessarily safe for drinking if adequately treated.

Be mindful of the water's current and depth. Even the most experienced swimmers can be caught off guard by sudden changes in depth or unexpected undercurrents. Avoid swimming in fast-moving rivers or streams, as these can quickly become dangerous. If you're unfamiliar with the area, ask locals or refer to guides about safe swimming spots.

It's also important to never swim alone. Having a buddy ensures that help is readily available in an emergency. Additionally, always inform someone on the shore of your swimming plans, including your expected return time.

Before entering the water, take a moment to acclimate to the temperature. Sudden immersion in cold water can lead to shock and hypothermia, impairing your ability to swim and make rational decisions. Gradually enter the water to allow your body to adjust.

Be cautious of wildlife. Many water bodies in the wilderness are home to snakes, leeches, and other potentially dangerous animals. Research the local wildlife and understand the risks before deciding to swim. Avoid areas known for harboring dangerous species.

Lastly, consider the impact of your swimming on the environment. If you plan to bathe, use biodegradable soap and avoid introducing foreign substances into the water. Remember, preserving the natural purity of wilderness water sources is essential for the health of the ecosystem and the safety of all who rely on it.

By adhering to these safe swimming practices, you can enjoy the refreshing and invigorating experience of swimming in the wild while minimizing risks to yourself and the environment. As we transition from understanding the risks associated with water to exploring strategies for staying hydrated in the wilderness, it's clear that water plays a multifaceted role in bushcraft and survival. Proper respect and understanding of this vital resource are critical to a safe and enjoyable wilderness experience.

Chapter Summary

- Finding and purifying water is crucial in the wilderness, as is recognizing signs of dehydration to prevent health issues.
- Initial signs of dehydration include thirst, dry mouth, fatigue, and decreased urine output. Urine color is a crucial indicator of hydration levels.
- Severe dehydration symptoms include headache, dizziness, dry skin, muscle cramps, confusion, rapid heartbeat, and fainting, necessitating immediate medical attention.
- Preventing dehydration involves starting well-hydrated, carrying sufficient water, and replenishing electrolytes, especially in hot, humid, or high-altitude conditions.
- Recognizing early signs of dehydration, such as a dry mouth and dark urine, is crucial in bushcraft and survival to prevent life-threatening emergencies.
- Treating waterborne illnesses involves staying hydrated, using oral rehydration solutions, and seeking medical attention for severe or persistent symptoms.

- Safe swimming practices in the wilderness include assessing water conditions, being cautious of wildlife, and minimizing environmental impact.

5
FOOD SAFETY AND NUTRITION

Two campers preparing food at a campsite.

Foraging for Edible Plants

Foraging for edible plants is a fundamental skill in bushcraft and survival, significantly enhancing food safety and nutrition. This skill involves identifying, harvesting, and preparing wild plants to supplement one's diet in the wilderness. It's essential to forage with respect for nature and understand the potential risks.

The first step in foraging is learning to identify edible plants accurately. Misidentification can lead to consuming toxic species, resulting in illness or worse. It's essential to familiarize yourself with the area's flora you'll be exploring by studying guidebooks, attending workshops, or participating in guided walks led by experienced foragers or botanists.

Start by focusing on a few easily recognizable and widely available plants, such as dandelions, which can be eaten entirely; nettles, which are excellent when cooked to remove their sting; and wild garlic, identifiable by its distinctive smell. The key to safe foraging is certainty; if you're not 100% sure of a plant's identity, do not eat it.

Sustainable harvesting practices are crucial to ensure that plant populations remain healthy and abundant for future foragers. It's advisable to take at most a third of what's available in a given area to preserve the ecosystem and allow plants to grow and propagate. Be mindful of the foraging location, avoid areas contaminated by pollutants, such as roadsides or industrial areas, and always wash plants thoroughly to remove dirt and potential pesticides.

Wild plants require specific preparation to be safe for

consumption, with some needing to be cooked to neutralize toxins. In contrast, others may only have certain edible parts. Researching and understanding the best practices for preparing each plant you intend to eat is essential. Incorporating wild plants into your diet can significantly enhance your nutritional intake, as many wild greens are rich in vitamins and minerals. However, it's essential to introduce new foods slowly and in small quantities to monitor for any adverse reactions.

While foraging can enrich your bushcraft experience, it comes with risks. Always carry a first aid kit and know how to use it. Learn to recognize the symptoms of allergic reactions and how to respond to them. Informing someone of your foraging plans and expected return is also wise, especially if venturing into remote areas.

In conclusion, foraging for edible plants offers a sustainable way to supplement your diet with nutritious food while engaging deeply with the natural environment. With the proper knowledge and respect for nature, it can be a safe and rewarding practice. As we move forward, enhancing our skills in hunting and fishing will further expand our capabilities for survival, providing additional means to secure food in the wilderness.

Hunting and Fishing for Survival

In bushcraft, procuring food through hunting and fishing is not only a skill but a necessity for survival. This section delves into the practical aspects of hunting and fishing for sustenance, emphasizing the importance of safety, nutrition, and the ethical considerations accompanying these primal activities.

Hunting in a survival situation requires a deep understanding of the local fauna, their habits, and the most humane and efficient hunting methods. It's crucial to familiarize oneself with the legalities surrounding hunting in the area, including seasons, licensing, and permissible take methods.

When hunting, always prioritize safety. This means personal safety and ensuring that your actions do not negatively impact the environment or local wildlife populations. Use weapons that you are trained and comfortable with, and always ensure a clean, ethical kill to prevent unnecessary suffering of the animal.

Nutritionally, wild game is an excellent source of lean protein, essential fats, and other nutrients. However, it's important to understand the preparation and cooking methods to preserve these nutrients while ensuring the meat is safe to consume. Different animals require different approaches to butchering and cooking, so knowledge and preparation are essential.

Similarly, fishing requires knowledge of the local aquatic species, habitats, and behaviors. Understanding the basics of sustainable fishing practices is essential to ensure that fish populations remain healthy for future generations.

When fishing for survival, consider the nutritional value of the fish you aim to catch. Fish are a rich source of omega-3 fatty acids, protein, and other vital nutrients. However, the preparation and cooking method can significantly affect their nutritional content. Aim for methods that preserve these nutrients, such as grilling or steaming rather than deep-frying.

Safety is also a paramount concern when fishing. This includes personal safety measures, such as being aware of the weather and water conditions, as well as the safety of the fish populations. Practice catch-and-release when appropriate, and be mindful of local size and bag limit regulations.

Ethics play a crucial role in hunting and fishing for survival. It's essential to approach these activities with respect for nature and the animals you're hunting or fishing. This means taking only what you need, minimizing waste, and ensuring your actions do not cause unnecessary harm or suffering.

In conclusion, hunting and fishing are invaluable skills in bushcraft and survival situations. They provide both a means of sustenance and a connection to the natural world. By approaching these activities with respect, knowledge, and preparation, one can ensure personal survival and the preservation of the natural environment and its inhabitants.

Preventing Foodborne Illnesses

The risk of foodborne illnesses increases in the wilderness, where modern food preservation and safety standards are not available. However, with the proper knowledge and precautions, these risks can be minimized, ensuring a safer and more enjoyable bushcraft experience. This section covers practical strategies for preventing foodborne illnesses by focusing on handling, preparing, and storing food in the wild.

Foodborne illnesses result from consuming contaminated food or beverages, with bacteria, viruses, parasites, or toxins being the usual culprits. Symptoms can range from mild discomfort to severe dehydration and, in extreme cases, death. In a survival situation, even a mild case can become dangerous if it leads to dehydration or impairs the ability to seek help or self-rescue.

To ensure safe food handling, washing hands and surfaces often is essential. If soap is unavailable, ash or sand can be used as alternatives. It's also crucial to keep all surfaces and utensils used for food preparation clean.

To avoid cross-contamination, separate cutting boards and knives should be used for raw meat and other foods, preventing the transfer of harmful bacteria. Cooking foods to safe temperatures is another critical practice; wild game should be cooked to an internal temperature of at least 165°F (74°C), and fish should be cooked until opaque and flaky.

When it comes to food storage, keeping cold foods cold and hot foods hot is essential. Perishable foods should be kept cool using natural refrigeration methods, such as submerging items in a cold stream or burying them in a cool, shaded area. Cooked food not consumed immediately should be kept hot to prevent bacterial growth or consumed as soon as possible if heating equipment is unavailable. Drying is an effective method for long-term storage of meats, fruits, and vegetables, ensuring they are thoroughly dried to prevent mold and bacterial growth.

Recognizing and choosing safe foods is also crucial. Correct identification is vital to avoid consuming toxic species when foraging for wild plants, fruits, or nuts. It's essential to use reliable field guides or the knowledge of experienced foragers. Similarly, caution should be exercised when selecting wild game and fish, avoiding animals that appear sick or behave abnormally and fish from polluted waters, which may carry diseases or harmful toxins.

In conclusion, preventing foodborne illnesses in the wilderness requires diligence and knowledge. Adhering to safe food handling, preparation, and storage practices can significantly reduce the risk of becoming ill. The goal is to survive and thrive in the natural environment, and maintaining good health through safe food practices is a critical component of bushcraft first aid.

Cooking and Preserving Wild Food

Understanding how to cook and preserve wild food safely is crucial in bushcraft for maintaining health and ensuring survival. This involves essential techniques and considerations for processing wild edibles, focusing on safety and nutritional preservation.

Cooking wild food enhances its flavor and is a critical step in eliminating potential pathogens. Thorough cooking of wild game, fish, or foraged plants is necessary, ensuring meats reach an internal temperature of at least 165°F (74°C) to destroy harmful bacteria like Salmonella and E. coli. Boiling plants for at least one minute can kill off most pathogens. However, some toxic plants require more specific treatment to neutralize their harmful components.

The cooking method is also essential; open fires are common in bushcraft but require careful management. Constructing a simple reflector oven from logs or rocks can help distribute heat more evenly. Using hot stones from the fire placed in a pit with the food and then covered with earth creates a makeshift oven that slowly cooks the food, preserving nutrients and reducing burning risks.

Preserving food for leaner times is a wise strategy when food is abundant. Various methods are available for preserving wild food, each with its advantages:

- **Drying** is an energy-efficient method, suitable for meat, fruits, vegetables, and herbs, especially in sunny, breezy locations or near a fire, ensuring thorough drying to prevent mold while avoiding over-drying.
- **Smoking** meat and fish preserves them and adds flavor, requiring a simple smoker setup and a low, consistent heat to avoid under-preservation.
- **Fermenting** extends shelf life and enhances nutritional value but requires knowledge of safe practices to avoid food poisoning.
- **Salting** draws out moisture to inhibit bacterial growth, with the challenge being to use enough salt for preservation without making the food too salty, followed by drying or smoking for additional preservation.

Hygiene is paramount, emphasizing clean hands, utensils, and surfaces to minimize contamination risks. Additionally, thoroughly understanding which plants and mushrooms are safe to eat is crucial, as some remain poisonous even after cooking or preservation. Mastering these techniques ensures a reliable food source in the wilderness, significantly contributing to health and survival in bushcraft situations.

Chapter Summary

- Foraging for edible plants is a crucial survival skill, requiring knowledge of plant identification, harvesting, and preparation to enhance food safety and nutrition.
- Misidentification of plants can lead to consuming toxic species; learning about local flora and focusing on easily recognizable plants like dandelions, nettles, and wild garlic is essential.
- Sustainable harvesting practices, such as taking no more than a third of available plants and avoiding contaminated areas, are crucial for ecosystem preservation.
- Many wild plants need specific preparation to be safe for consumption, and incorporating

them into your diet can significantly improve nutritional intake.

- Hunting and fishing for survival require understanding local fauna, legalities, safety, and ethical considerations, emphasizing minimizing environmental impact and animal suffering.
- Preventing foodborne illnesses in the wilderness involves safe food handling, preparation, and storage practices, including washing hands, avoiding cross-contamination, and cooking foods to safe temperatures.
- Cooking and preserving wild food safely is paramount, and techniques like drying, smoking, fermenting, and salting are vital for eliminating pathogens and extending food's shelf life.

6

SHELTER AND EXPOSURE PROTECTION

Shelter built into a tree.

Choosing a Safe Shelter Location

In bushcraft first aid, understanding how to choose a safe shelter location is paramount for survival and protection against the elements. This decision can significantly impact your ability to maintain body heat, stay dry, and avoid potential hazards. The following guidelines are designed to help you select an optimal site for your shelter, ensuring your safety and comfort in wilderness settings.

First and foremost, look for natural protection from the elements. This could be a rock overhang, a dense stand of trees, or a depression in the ground. These features can provide essential shelter from wind, rain, and snow, reducing the need for extensive shelter construction. However, it's crucial to assess the stability of these natural shelters to avoid any risk of collapse or flooding.

Elevation is another critical factor to consider. While setting up camp in a low-lying area near a water source might seem appealing, these locations are prone to cold air pools at night, which can significantly lower the temperature. Furthermore, valleys and depressions are at a higher risk of flooding. Instead, seek out a flat spot on higher ground, ensuring it's not at the peak where you would be exposed to strong winds.

Proximity to water is essential for hydration, cooking, and hygiene. However, establishing your shelter too close to water bodies can lead to problems. Apart from the flooding risk, areas near water attract insects and wildlife. A distance of about 60-100 meters from a water source strikes a good balance between convenience and safety.

Consideration of potential hazards is crucial. Avoid areas with a risk of falling rocks or branches, which can be identified by looking for debris on the ground. Also, steer clear of animal paths to reduce the likelihood of unwanted encounters with wildlife. Inspecting the area for signs of insects, such as ant hills or wasp nests, is also advisable to prevent uncomfortable or dangerous situations.

Lastly, the orientation of your shelter can play a significant role in your comfort and survival. In colder climates, positioning the entrance away from prevailing winds while capturing morning sunlight can help warm the shelter. In warmer regions, maximizing ventilation and shade will be more beneficial to avoid overheating.

By carefully assessing these factors, you can choose a shelter location that offers safety, comfort, and protection. This strategic selection is the first step in ensuring your well-being in the wilderness, setting a solid foundation for constructing insulated shelters and other survival tactics covered in bushcraft first aid.

Building Insulated Shelters

When selecting an appropriate location for your shelter, it's crucial to ensure your safety and comfort in the wilderness by constructing a shelter that provides adequate insulation. Insulation is essential for protection against the cold, retaining body heat, and even shielding you from the heat in warmer climates. This section will help you build insulated shelters using materials commonly found in the wilderness.

First, you need to gather the materials for insulation and structure. Dry leaves, moss, pine needles, and small branches are excellent for insulation as they trap air, a poor conductor of heat, thereby retaining warmth within the shelter. For the shelter's structure, search for larger branches, fallen trees, or natural features like a rock face that can serve as the backbone of your construction.

Begin constructing your shelter by setting up the framework. If you're utilizing a fallen tree or a rock face as a base, arrange large branches at an angle to create a lean-to structure. It's essential to ensure that the framework is sturdy enough to support the weight of the insulating materials and any additional snow or debris that may accumulate.

Once the framework is established, add your insulating materials from the bottom up, layering leaves, moss, and pine needles. The effectiveness of the insulation increases with its thickness; aim for a minimum thickness of 12 inches (30 cm) on all sides of the shelter, including the ground. Placing branches over the insulation as you progress can help keep it in place and add an extra layer of protection against the elements.

After insulating the shelter, inspect it for gaps or holes where the wind could penetrate and use additional insulating materials to fill them. The entrance of your shelter requires special attention to reduce heat loss; consider creating a small hallway or positioning the entrance away from the prevailing wind.

Before settling in for the night, test the shelter's insulation by spending a short period inside with the entrance sealed. If you notice any drafts, reinforce these areas with more insulation. The effectiveness of your shelter's insulation is crucial for a comfortable and safe night.

Maintain your shelter throughout your stay. Insulation materials may settle or compress, reducing their effectiveness. Regularly fluff up the insulation and add more materials as needed. After any wind or snow, check the shelter for damage and make necessary repairs.

Following these steps can significantly increase your comfort and safety in the wilderness. Remember, the key to effective insulation is thickness and coverage, so ensure your shelter is well-insulated on all sides, including the ground, to protect against the cold and retain body heat.

Protecting Yourself from the Elements

In the wilderness, your ability to find or create shelter is your first line of defense against the harsh elements. However, there will be times when you're exposed to the elements, either while moving between shelters or when a shelter isn't immediately available. Protecting yourself from wind, rain, snow, and sun is crucial for your survival and well-being. This involves practical strategies to shield yourself from the adverse effects of exposure.

To protect against wind, which can strip away the warm air your body maintains around itself and increase the risk of hypothermia, use natural terrain features like rocks, trees, or depressions to break the wind's force. If moving, orient your body and backpack to minimize exposure to the wind. A windbreak made from branches, a tarp, or snow can provide temporary relief.

Rain can lead to discomfort, hypothermia, or trench foot if not appropriately managed. Waterproof clothing is essential, but in its absence, a poncho or tarp can serve as a makeshift raincoat or shelter. When setting up camp, look for a location with a natural overhead cover or elevation to avoid water pooling. Keeping dry is crucial, so wring out wet clothing and dry it by a fire or in the sun whenever possible.

Snow poses a unique challenge as it can insulate and

induce hypothermia. Use snow to your advantage by building a shelter like a quinzhee or snow cave for insulation. If on the move, layer your clothing to keep warm air close to your body and prevent snow from melting into your layers by waterproofing your outer layer. Avoid sweating to reduce heat loss.

Sun exposure can lead to dehydration, sunburn, and heatstroke. Protect your skin with clothing, hats, and sunscreen. Use sunglasses or improvised eyewear to prevent snow blindness in snowy environments. Seek shade during the hottest parts of the day and travel during cooler hours if necessary. A simple shade shelter can offer temporary relief during rest stops.

Several general principles apply regardless of the element you're facing. Stay hydrated and well-fed to maintain resilience against extreme temperatures. Layer your clothing to quickly adjust to changing conditions and be prepared to improvise with what you have. Your mental attitude plays a significant role in your physical well-being, so stay calm, assess your situation logically, and take decisive action to protect yourself from the elements.

Understanding and applying these strategies can significantly increase your chances of staying safe and healthy in the wilderness, even under challenging environmental conditions.

Fire Safety and Warmth

Mastering the art of creating and maintaining a fire is crucial in the wilderness, as it serves as a lifeline. Fire not only provides warmth and light but also enables the cooking of food and the purification of water and can be vital in signaling for help. Alongside its numerous benefits, it's important to practice fire safety to prevent injuries and protect the environment. This section will walk you through the essentials of safely utilizing fire's life-saving benefits.

When selecting a location for your fire, it's essential to choose a spot sheltered from the wind yet with good ventilation to prevent smoke inhalation. Avoid areas close to trees, bushes, and other flammable materials to reduce the risk of the fire spreading. Clear a wide area on the soil, removing any leaves, twigs, and debris that could catch fire. If possible, use a fire pit surrounded by rocks to help contain the fire.

Before lighting your fire, you must gather three materials: tinder, kindling, and fuel. Tinder includes small, easily ignitable items such as dry leaves, grass, or twigs. Kindling consists of slightly larger sticks that can catch fire from the tinder, and fuel is made up of larger pieces of wood that will keep the fire burning for longer. Arrange these materials nearby so they can be added to the fire as needed, but ensure they are not so close as to catch fire from a stray spark.

Always opt for a safe ignition source for lighting the fire, like matches or a lighter. In damp conditions, waterproof matches or a fire starter may be necessary. Avoid using flammable liquids such as gasoline, as they can lead to uncontrollable flames and serious injuries. Begin by lighting the tinder and then gently add kindling as the fire grows, followed by the larger pieces of fuel. Keeping the fire manageable is essential to meet your needs without becoming a hazard.

To maintain your fire, add fuel as needed, but ensure it doesn't grow too large. Always have water or soil on hand to extinguish the fire if necessary. It's crucial never to leave your fire unattended, as a sudden gust of wind could cause the flames to spread. When extinguishing the fire, do so gradually by sprinkling water or covering it with soil, then stir the ashes to make sure no embers remain that could reignite.

Despite taking all precautions, accidents can happen, and burns may occur. Cool the area with clean water for minor burns, and cover it with a sterile dressing. Seek medical attention immediately for more severe burns. Always keep a first aid kit nearby when handling fire.

Lastly, it's important to practice Leave No Trace principles to minimize the impact of your fire on the environment. Use existing fire rings when available and ensure your fire is completely extinguished and cold to the touch before leaving the site. To further reduce impact, scatter cool ashes over a wide area away from the campsite.

By adhering to these guidelines, you can enjoy the numerous benefits of a fire while ensuring your safety and the protection of the wilderness. Fire is a powerful tool in bushcraft and survival but requires respect and responsibility.

Chapter Summary

- Choose a shelter site with natural cover, such as rock overhangs or dense trees, on high ground away from water to prevent flooding, and position it to suit the climate.
- Build the shelter using dry leaves, moss, and branches for insulation, aiming for at least 12 inches of thickness for warmth and sealing gaps against the wind.
- Use the landscape and items like tarps to shield against wind, rain, and snow, and wear appropriate clothing and sunscreen for sun protection.
- For fire safety, pick a sheltered, airy spot away from flammables, prepare with tinder,

kindling, and fuel, keep the fire small, and ensure it's fully extinguished afterward.

- Maintain hydration and nutrition, adjust clothing layers for temperature, use what's available for improvisation, and stay calm and logical in problem-solving.
- Follow Leave No Trace principles to minimize environmental impact, use existing fire rings, and scatter cooled ashes.
- Survival hinges on good insulation, element protection, fire safety, and effective signaling, highlighting the importance of preparation, improvisation, and environmental respect.

7

NAVIGATING MENTAL HEALTH CHALLENGES

An adventurer dealing with stress in the wilderness.

Coping with Stress and Anxiety

In the wilderness, where the unpredictability of nature meets the solitude of the untamed, stress and anxiety can become as challenging as any physical obstacle. The key to coping with these mental health challenges lies in understanding their roots and employing practical strategies to mitigate their impact.

First and foremost, it's essential to recognize the signs of stress and anxiety. These can manifest in various ways, including increased heart rate, restlessness, difficulty concentrating, and irritability. Acknowledging these symptoms early on is the first step towards managing them effectively.

Establishing a routine is one effective strategy for coping with stress and anxiety in bushcraft situations. The wilderness's unpredictability can be overwhelming, but a routine provides a sense of control and normalcy. This could be as simple as setting up camp before dusk, gathering water at dawn, or allocating specific meal times. Such predictability can be a comforting anchor amid chaos.

Another vital technique is mindfulness and grounding exercises. When anxiety strikes, grounding oneself in the present moment can help mitigate overwhelming feelings. Techniques such as deep breathing, mindfulness meditation, or even focusing on the sensory experiences of the wilderness (the sound of a nearby stream, the smell of pine, the feel of the earth beneath your feet) can help calm the mind and reduce anxiety levels.

Physical activity is also a powerful tool for managing stress and anxiety. Bushcraft inherently involves physical tasks, but it's important to engage in these activities mindfully, focusing on the movement and the environment rather than as a mere survival chore. This not only helps expend pent-up energy but also boosts endorphin levels, improving mood and reducing stress.

Even in a solitary bushcraft scenario, social support should be considered. Open communication about feelings and experiences can provide a sense of shared understanding and support if you're with a group. If you're alone, keeping a journal or speaking aloud about your thoughts and feelings can offer a form of emotional release and reflection.

Lastly, setting realistic goals and celebrating small achievements can significantly boost morale. In a bushcraft context, this could mean successfully starting a fire with damp wood, finding a water source, or building a shelter that withstands the night. These achievements provide tangible evidence of progress and capability, which can be incredibly uplifting in moments of doubt.

In conclusion, coping with stress and anxiety in bushcraft requires a multifaceted approach that encompasses physical, emotional, and psychological strategies. By recognizing the signs, establishing routines, practicing mindfulness, engaging in physical activity, seeking social support, and celebrating small victories, one can navigate the mental challenges of the wilderness with resilience and grace.

The Psychological Impact of Survival Situations

Survival situations exert a profound psychological impact on individuals. The stress of navigating the unknown, coupled with the physical demands of bushcraft, can significantly affect one's mental health. Understanding this impact is crucial for anyone venturing into the wilderness, as it is the first step toward maintaining psychological well-being in challenging environments.

The initial reaction to a survival situation often involves a surge of adrenaline. This fight-or-flight response can provide the necessary energy to deal with immediate threats. However, this state could be more sustainable in the long term. Once the initial shock wears off, the reality of the situation sets in, and individuals may experience a wide range of emotions, including fear, anxiety, frustration, and despair. These feelings are natural responses to wilderness survival's uncertainty and potential dangers.

One of the most significant psychological impacts of survival situations is the sense of loss of control. People are accustomed to having a certain degree of control over their environment and outcomes in everyday life. In the wilderness, however, many variables are beyond one's control, such as weather conditions, availability of resources, and potential hazards. This loss of control can lead to feelings of helplessness and vulnerability, which, if not addressed, can escalate into more severe mental health issues, such as depression or acute stress disorder.

Moreover, the isolation often experienced in survival scenarios can exacerbate these psychological challenges. Humans are inherently social creatures; lacking social interaction can lead to loneliness and disconnection. This isolation can hinder one's ability to maintain a positive outlook. It can impair decision-making abilities, as no one can discuss options or strategies with.

To mitigate these psychological impacts, it is essential to develop coping strategies that can help maintain mental resilience. Simple techniques, such as setting small, achievable goals, practicing mindfulness, and focusing on the tasks, can provide a sense of control and purpose. Additionally, even in the wilderness, maintaining a routine can offer a semblance of normalcy and stability, comforting in times of stress.

Acknowledging and accepting the emotions that arise in survival situations is also essential. Suppressing or denying feelings of fear or anxiety can lead to increased stress and mental fatigue. Instead, recognizing these emotions as natural responses to the circumstances allows individuals to address them constructively by adjusting their approach to the situation or using relaxation techniques to manage stress.

In conclusion, the psychological impact of survival situations is a critical aspect of bushcraft first aid that requires as much attention as physical injuries. By understanding the mental challenges that may arise and equipping oneself with strategies to cope with them, individuals can enhance their resilience and improve their chances of surviving and thriving in the wilderness. The journey through the mental landscape of survival is as demanding as the physical trek. Still, with the proper preparation and mindset, it is possible to navigate this terrain successfully.

Building Resilience and Mental Toughness

Understanding the psychological impact of survival situations is crucial, as is developing the resilience and mental toughness needed to navigate these challenges effectively. It's not just about enduring; it's about adapting and thriving in adversity. Practical strategies and techniques to fortify mental resilience are essential for anyone venturing into the wilderness or engaging in bushcraft activities.

A positive mindset is fundamental to resilience, focusing on solutions rather than problems and viewing challenges as opportunities for growth. Practicing gratitude by acknowledging what you are thankful for daily, even in difficult situations, can shift your focus from what's lacking to what's abundant, fostering a more positive outlook.

Setting achievable goals provides direction and a sense of purpose, such as building a shelter or finding water in a survival situation. Achieving these goals boosts morale and motivates you to tackle the next challenge.

Stress is inevitable, but maintaining mental toughness is critical. Techniques like deep breathing, meditation, and mindfulness can calm the mind and reduce anxiety, preparing you to handle stress more effectively when it arises.

Problem-solving is a critical resilience skill. It involves identifying problems, brainstorming solutions, evaluating them, and implementing the most viable ones. Practicing problem-solving can make you more adept at handling unexpected challenges.

A robust support system provides emotional strength and encouragement, offering valuable insights and coping strategies. In survival contexts, working effectively as a team enhances problem-solving capabilities and provides mutual support.

Resilience involves learning from failure and viewing each setback as an opportunity to grow. Reflecting on what went wrong and how to improve turns failure from a discouragement source into a stepping stone toward success.

Physical and mental resilience are interconnected; regular exercise improves health, reduces stress, and enhances mental toughness. Incorporating physical training into preparation for bushcraft activities can significantly bolster resilience.

Visualizing yourself successfully navigating challenges, a technique known as mental rehearsal, prepares your mind for the challenges ahead, making you more confident and resilient. Building resilience and mental toughness is a continuous process that requires practice and dedication.

By incorporating these strategies into your preparation and mindset, you can enhance your ability to navigate the mental health challenges of survival situations, ensuring your survival and your ability to thrive in the face of adversity.

Chapter Summary

- Recognize signs of stress and anxiety in wilderness situations, such as increased heart rate and difficulty concentrating.

- Establish a routine to provide a sense of control and normalcy amidst the unpredictability of the wilderness.
- To mitigate anxiety, practice mindfulness and grounding exercises like deep breathing and focusing on sensory experiences.
- Exercise to manage stress, boost endorphins, and improve mood.
- Seek social support through open communication or journaling to share feelings and experiences.
- Set realistic goals and celebrate small achievements to boost morale and provide evidence of progress.
- Maintain morale and hope by establishing routines, setting achievable goals, and staying connected with nature.
- Build resilience and mental toughness through cultivating a positive mindset, managing stress, developing problem-solving skills, and learning from failure.

8

EMERGENCY SIGNALING AND RESCUE

A man lighting a flare in the wilderness.

Creating Effective Signals

In bushcraft and wilderness survival, creating effective signals for rescue is paramount. This skill can significantly increase your chances of being found by rescuers in an emergency. The key to successful signaling lies in understanding and utilizing three primary principles: visibility, audibility, and repetition.

Visibility is your foremost ally in the wilderness. To create obvious signals, consider using bright colors, especially those that starkly contrast the natural environment. For instance, orange, red, and neon colors are particularly effective. One method is to use a brightly colored fabric or an emergency blanket to create a large, noticeable sign on the ground or to hang it from a tree. The international distress signal, which consists of three of anything (three fires, three piles of rocks, and three pieces of fabric), is a universally recognized sign for help. Arranging these signals in an open area can enhance their visibility from the air.

Reflective materials can also play a crucial role in signaling for help. Mirrors or any reflective surface can catch the sun's rays and signal to aircraft. The key is to aim the reflection toward the potential rescuer, using the "flash" of light to grab attention. This method requires sunlight, so it's essential to consider the time of day and weather conditions when planning to use this technique.

Audibility complements visibility in emergency signaling. Sound can be your best signaling tool in environments where visibility is limited, such as dense forests or at night. Whistles are excellent for this purpose as they can produce a loud, piercing sound that can travel long distances. Three blasts of a whistle, repeated at regular intervals, is a recognized distress signal. Banging metal objects together or using a horn can also create effective auditory signals.

Repetition is the third principle of effective signaling. A signal is more likely to be noticed if repeated at regular intervals. This applies to both visual and auditory signals. For visual signals, ensure they are maintained and visible until rescue arrives. For auditory signals, set a schedule for producing the sound, such as every hour, to increase the chances of being heard by rescuers.

Remember, creating effective signals aims to make it as easy as possible for rescuers to locate you. Applying these principles can significantly improve your chances of a successful rescue in an emergency. Always be prepared to use whatever materials you have at your disposal and think creatively to enhance the effectiveness of your signals.

Using Technology for Rescue

In the wilderness, where the beauty of nature meets the unpredictability of outdoor adventures, the importance of preparedness cannot be overstated. While traditional signaling methods play a crucial role in emergencies, technology has introduced a new layer of safety and efficiency in rescue operations. This section delves into the use of technology for rescue, providing practical advice on how to leverage modern devices and services to ensure your safety in the great outdoors.

Personal Locator Beacons (PLBs): A Personal Locator Beacon is a compact device designed to send an SOS signal to your location to search and rescue services. When activated, a PLB transmits a distress signal to the nearest search and rescue satellite system, relaying your position and information to local search and rescue teams. It's essential for adventurers venturing into remote areas where cell service is nonexistent. Ensure your PLB is registered with your details for a swift response in an emergency.

Satellite Messengers: These devices offer two-way communication capabilities, allowing you to send and receive text messages via satellite networks. In addition to SOS functions similar to PLBs, satellite messengers enable you to communicate with family, friends, or emergency services, even from the most remote locations. Some models also allow for weather updates and navigation features, making them a versatile tool for bushcraft enthusiasts.

Smartphone Apps: In areas with cellular coverage, several smartphone applications can enhance your safety. Apps designed for outdoor adventures can provide GPS navigation, weather alerts, and even the ability to share your real-time location with trusted contacts. While relying solely on a smartphone is not advisable due to battery life constraints and potential lack of signal, these apps can be valuable to your safety toolkit when used appropriately.

Emergency Signal Mirrors and Whistles: Though not electronic, these tools are worth mentioning for their simplicity and effectiveness in conjunction with technology. Under the right conditions, an emergency signal mirror can catch the attention of rescuers from miles away, while a whistle can be heard over long distances when visibility is poor or in densely wooded areas. Both items should be a staple in any bushcraft first aid kit as a backup to your technological devices.

Preparation and Practice: Regardless of the technology you choose to carry, familiarizing yourself with its operation before embarking on your adventure is crucial. Practice using your devices in various conditions to ensure you can operate them effectively in an emergency. Additionally, inform someone of your planned route and expected return time, providing them with instructions on what to do if you fail to check-in.

In conclusion, integrating technology into your bushcraft first aid and rescue toolkit offers a significant advantage in ensuring safety and facilitating rescue in emergencies. By combining traditional signaling methods with modern technology, you can enjoy the wilderness with the confidence that help is within reach should you need it. As we move forward, the next section will guide you through navigational aids and techniques, further equipping you with the knowledge to navigate the wilderness safely and efficiently.

Navigational Aids and Techniques

In bushcraft and wilderness survival, effectively navigating through the wilderness is not just a skill—it's essential for survival. Beyond the basic knowledge of using a map and compass, numerous navigational aids and techniques can significantly improve your chances of being rescued or finding your way back to safety. This section explores these vital tools and methods, aiming to equip you with the skills needed to navigate emergencies in the wilderness.

Nature offers various navigational aids for those who know how to interpret them. The sun, stars, and even the growth patterns of moss on trees can provide directional clues. For example, in the Northern Hemisphere, the sun's path from east to west can help establish an east-west orientation. At the same time, the North Star (Polaris) indicates north at night. These natural indicators are invaluable in the absence of compasses or GPS devices.

Another helpful skill is creating an improvised

compass. This can be done by magnetizing a needle by rubbing it against silk or wool and then floating it on a leaf in still water. The needle will align with the Earth's magnetic field, indicating the north-south line. Although more accurate than a standard compass, this method can offer a crucial directional reference when needed.

Understanding how to read topographical maps is also crucial. These maps show paths and roads and detail the terrain, including hills, valleys, and bodies of water. Learning to interpret contour lines and symbols can aid in navigating through challenging landscapes and identifying potential locations for rescue signals. Combining map knowledge with land navigation skills, such as triangulation using visible landmarks, can significantly improve your ability to move purposefully toward safety or to signal for help effectively.

The importance of GPS devices and satellite messengers in navigation cannot be overstated. These tools provide precise location data, making it easier for rescuers to find you. Many of these devices also allow sending distress signals and messages from remote locations where traditional communication methods are ineffective.

Marking your path when moving is crucial for helping rescuers track your movements and preventing you from circling back on yourself. Creating noticeable but environmentally friendly markers using natural materials, as well as understanding how to leave clear, universal distress signals, can facilitate search teams' efforts to locate you.

A key aspect of navigation is not just finding your way but also "staying found." This involves making informed decisions about when to move and when to stay put to increase your visibility to rescuers. Establishing a visible campsite, using bright materials, or creating smoke signals can make it easier for search teams to find you.

In conclusion, mastering navigational aids and techniques is critical to bushcraft first aid and emergency preparedness. From recognizing natural cues to leveraging modern technology, these skills enable confident navigation through the wilderness. As we move forward, the focus will shift to effectively interacting with rescuers, ensuring that once found, you can communicate your needs and understand their instructions, completing the rescue process efficiently and safely.

Interacting with Rescuers

Interacting with rescuers is critical in any survival situation in the wilderness. After successfully signaling for help using the techniques and navigational aids discussed, the focus shifts to ensuring a safe and effective handover to the rescue team. This section delves into the best practices for interacting with rescuers, emphasizing clear communication, understanding rescue operations, and preparing for evacuation.

First and foremost, it's vital to remain visible and make it easy for rescuers to reach you. If you've used signals to attract attention, maintain those signals as long as possible or until rescuers signal you to stop. This could mean burning a fire, leaving a signal mirror in a visible location, or using signaling devices.

Once rescuers are in sight, follow their instructions carefully. They may guide you verbally or use hand signals, especially if they are approaching from a helicopter and the noise makes communication difficult. If you're in a group, designate one person to communicate with the rescuers to avoid confusion.

It's also important to inform the rescuers of any medical emergencies or injuries within your group. Be prepared to quickly and accurately describe the nature of the injuries, any first aid administered, and the current condition of the injured party. This information is crucial for rescuers to prioritize medical attention and allocate resources effectively.

It is essential to understand that rescue operations may take time to set up, especially in challenging terrain. Rescuers must assess the situation, possibly secure the area, and determine the safest extraction method. During this time, remain calm, stay in place unless instructed otherwise, and keep your group together.

Preparing for evacuation involves several key steps. Gather all your gear and be ready to move on short notice. If there are injured individuals, ensure they are as comfortable and stable as possible for transport. Listen to the rescuers' instructions on assisting in the evacuation process, whether that involves helping to carry the injured, following a specific path, or boarding a rescue vehicle in an orderly manner.

Lastly, once you are in the care of the rescue team, trust their expertise and follow their guidance. They are trained professionals equipped to handle wilderness rescues. They will take the necessary steps to ensure your safety and well-being.

Interacting with rescuers effectively can significantly impact the outcome of a rescue operation. By staying visible, communicating clearly, and following instructions, you can aid in a smooth and efficient rescue process, paving the way for a safe evacuation from the wilderness.

Preparing for Evacuation

In the wilderness, the moment you realize that evacuation is necessary, whether due to injury, severe weather, or any other critical situation, your preparation for a safe extraction begins. This preparation is a multifaceted process that involves both physical and mental readiness, ensuring that when rescuers arrive, you are ready to leave promptly and safely.

1. **Gather Essential Items:** Assemble a small, lightweight pack of essential items. This should include a first aid kit, personal medication, a water bottle, high-energy food bars, a flashlight or headlamp with extra batteries, a whistle, a compact emergency blanket, and a multi-tool. If possible, include a copy of your identification and any relevant medical information. This pack should be easily accessible and ready to grab at a moment's notice.

2. **Mark Your Location:** While waiting for rescue, make your location visible from the air and ground. Use bright materials or reflective items, or create signals on the ground using rocks or logs that contrast with the natural environment. If you have a fire, consider creating smoke signals by adding green vegetation to the fire to produce thick smoke during the day. At night, a fire itself can be a powerful signal.

3. **Prepare Physically and Mentally:** Depending on the nature of the emergency, physical preparation might involve dressing appropriately for the weather or terrain, staying hydrated and nourished, or administering first aid to yourself or others. Mental preparation is equally

important. Stay calm, maintain a positive outlook, and mentally rehearse what you will say and do when rescuers arrive. This includes knowing your location as precisely as possible, understanding the nature of your emergency, and being able to communicate any immediate medical needs.

4. Secure Your Immediate Surroundings: Ensure your immediate area is safe and accessible for rescuers. This might involve clearing a landing zone for a helicopter, marking a clear path to your location if in a dense forest, or making sure that the area around you is stable and not prone to sudden flooding, rockslides, or other hazards.

5. Conserve Your Phone Battery: If you have a cell phone with you, conserve its battery life as much as possible. Turn off non-essential apps, reduce screen brightness, and switch to airplane mode when not in use. Your phone could be your lifeline to communicate with rescuers, especially if you can send GPS coordinates or other critical information.

6. Stay Put Unless Necessary: Once you have signaled for help and are awaiting rescue, it's generally best to stay in your current location unless you have a good reason to move. Moving can make it harder for rescuers to find you, especially if you leave after signaling your location. If you must move, leave clear, unmistakable signs of your direction of travel.

7. Be Ready to Assist Rescuers: When rescuers arrive, be prepared to follow their instructions immediately. They may require your assistance in making the evacuation smoother or faster, such as by helping to carry equipment or moving to a more accessible location for extraction.

By meticulously preparing for evacuation, you increase your chances of a successful rescue and contribute to the operation's safety and efficiency. Remember, your preparation can significantly impact the outcome, so take these steps seriously and ensure you are as ready as possible when help arrives.

Chapter Summary

- Effective emergency signaling in wilderness survival relies on visibility, audibility, and repetition, using bright colors, loud sounds, and repeated signals to attract rescuers.
- Brightly colored fabrics, reflective materials, and the international distress signal of three of anything (fires, rocks, fabrics) enhance visibility for aerial rescue.
- Auditory signals like whistle blasts, banging metal objects, or using a horn can

complement visual signals, especially in low-visibility conditions.

- Personal Locator Beacons (PLBs) and Satellite Messengers are crucial for sending SOS signals and enabling two-way communication in remote areas without cell service.
- Smartphone apps can provide GPS navigation, weather alerts, and real-time location sharing. Still, they should not be solely relied upon due to battery and signal limitations.
- Essential preparation steps include familiarity with device operation, informing someone of your route and expected return, and carrying non-electronic signaling tools like mirrors and whistles.
- Navigational skills, including using natural cues, improvised compasses, topographical maps, and path marking, are vital for moving toward safety or enhancing signal visibility.
- Preparing for evacuation involves gathering essential items, making your location visible, conserving phone battery, and being ready to assist rescuers for a smooth and efficient rescue operation.

9
WEATHER AND ENVIRONMENTAL HAZARDS

Rainy weather in the wilderness.

Understanding Weather Patterns

In bushcraft, a profound understanding of weather patterns is a cornerstone for ensuring safety and preparedness in the wilderness. With its inherent unpredictability and potential for rapid change, weather poses a significant environmental hazard that can impact health, safety, and the ability to navigate or remain in the wilderness. This section delves into the critical aspects of weather patterns, equipping you with the knowledge to anticipate and respond to various environmental conditions.

Weather patterns, fundamentally, are the varying atmospheric conditions that occur over some time in a particular area. These patterns range from clear skies and mild temperatures to severe storms and extreme temperatures. Recognizing the signs of changing weather can differentiate between a successful outing and a potentially dangerous situation.

First and foremost, understanding the basics of weather systems is essential. High and low-pressure systems, fronts, and other meteorological terms are not just for forecasters but are crucial for anyone venturing into the wilderness. High-pressure systems typically bring fair weather, while low-pressure systems can lead to poor weather, including storms and rain. Recognizing the signs of these systems can give you a heads-up before changes occur.

Cloud formations and types offer significant clues about impending weather. For instance, cumulonimbus clouds are often harbingers of thunderstorms. In contrast, high and wispy cirrus clouds may indicate a change in the weather within the next 24 hours. Understanding these patterns allows for better planning and decision-making while in the bush.

Wind direction and speed can also provide insights into upcoming weather. Sudden changes in wind direction or an increase in wind speed can signify a change in weather patterns, potentially heralding the approach of a storm. By paying attention to the wind, you can often anticipate shifts in weather that could impact your activities.

Temperature fluctuations, especially sudden drops, can indicate the approach of colder weather or a storm front. Being attuned to these changes is vital, especially when considering the risks of hypothermia or other cold-related conditions in the wilderness.

Barometric pressure, measured by a barometer, is another critical tool for understanding weather patterns. A falling barometer indicates worsening weather, while a rising barometer suggests improving conditions. This tool can be invaluable for predicting weather changes quickly, allowing for timely adjustments to plans and activities.

Finally, the natural world itself provides cues about the weather. Animals, insects, and plants exhibit behavior changes that can signal weather changes. Birds flying low, for instance, can indicate bad weather approaching, as can the increased activity of ants or bees.

In summary, a comprehensive understanding of weather patterns is indispensable for anyone engaging in bushcraft. By becoming familiar with the signs and signals of changing weather, you can make informed decisions that enhance your safety and enjoyment of the wilderness. This knowledge prepares you for the challenges of the environment. It deepens your connection with nature, allowing for a more harmonious and respectful interaction with the wild.

Preparing for Extreme Weather Conditions

In bushcraft, being prepared for extreme weather conditions is crucial for comfort, survival, and safety. The unpredictability of weather, especially in wilderness areas, can quickly transform an adventure into a problematic situation. Practical strategies and essential knowledge are vital to navigate these conditions effectively.

Extreme weather can take various forms, such as severe storms, extreme heat, freezing temperatures, and sudden weather changes, each presenting unique challenges. Severe storms may cause flooding and falling trees, extreme heat can lead to dehydration and heatstroke, and freezing temperatures increase the risk of hypothermia and frostbite.

The right gear acts as the first line of defense against extreme weather. Clothing should be versatile, allowing for layering to adjust to changing conditions. Investing in quality, weather-appropriate clothing that adheres to layering principles—base layers for moisture management, insulating layers for warmth, and outer layers for wind and water protection—is essential. Carrying a well-constructed, all-weather shelter, such as a tarp or a bivvy sack, can be crucial in unexpected conditions.

Choosing the right camp location is also critical. Avoid low-lying areas that could flood during heavy rains and seek natural shelters against strong winds. In hot conditions, prioritize shade and airflow; in cold environments, seek protection from the wind. Knowing how to construct and where to place emergency shelters can significantly enhance your safety in adverse conditions.

Maintaining hydration and energy is vital in extreme weather. Increase water intake in hot weather to avoid dehydration and up your calorie intake in cold conditions as your body uses more energy to stay warm. Always carry a means to purify water and have a reliable method to melt snow if necessary.

Monitoring the health of yourself and your

companions is crucial. Be aware of the signs of hypothermia, heatstroke, dehydration, and frostbite. A well-stocked first aid kit tailored to the environment and your group's needs is essential, as is proficiency in its use to prevent minor issues from becoming life-threatening.

Advanced planning and weather awareness are essential. Research the weather patterns of your destination and be prepared for unexpected changes. It is also beneficial to develop the skill to read natural weather indicators, such as cloud formations, wind direction, and temperature shifts.

Lastly, the importance of training and continuous skills development must be considered. Attending courses, practicing regularly, and seeking to learn more about surviving in extreme weather conditions are crucial. Knowledge and preparation are your best tools in the wilderness, significantly increasing your safety and enjoyment outdoors. The goal is to survive and thrive, regardless of the challenges posed by Mother Nature.

Avoiding Natural Hazards

In the wilderness, the unpredictability of nature often presents a variety of hazards that can pose significant risks to your health and safety. Understanding how to avoid these natural hazards is crucial for any bushcraft enthusiast. Practical strategies and knowledge are essential for navigating through and mitigating the risks posed by environmental hazards.

Rivers, lakes, and streams are vital water sources but can also be treacherous. Before crossing any body of water, it's essential to continually assess the current, depth, and potential obstacles. Using a stick to gauge depth and stability can be helpful.

When crossing a river, it is advisable to choose a wide, shallow section and face upstream, leaning slightly into the current for stability. Being informed about local weather conditions and avoiding camping in flood-prone zones can help you avoid flash floods, especially in canyons and low-lying areas.

Navigating rugged terrain and dense vegetation can be challenging and may conceal potential dangers. Maintaining a steady pace and using a stick or machete to clear a path if necessary can help. It's also important to be mindful of hidden obstacles like holes, sharp rocks, and thorny plants that can cause injuries. Wearing high boots and thick trousers can offer additional protection in areas known for snakes or other dangerous wildlife.

Encounters with wildlife can be thrilling but sometimes dangerous. Educating yourself about the local fauna and learning how to react in the event of an encounter is crucial. Making noise while hiking can help avoid surprising bears, and avoiding sudden movements is important when encountering snakes. Securing your food correctly is essential to avoid attracting animals to your campsite.

Sudden weather changes can expose you to hypothermia, heatstroke, and lightning strikes. Dressing in layers to adapt to changing temperatures and always carrying waterproof gear are good practices. In hot weather, staying hydrated, seeking shade during the hottest part of the day, and recognizing the signs of heat-related illnesses are important.

If caught in a thunderstorm, avoid open fields, high ground, and tall, isolated trees. It is advisable to find shelter in a low area but avoid depressions that can quickly fill with water.

While fire is a crucial survival tool, it's also a potential hazard. Essential safety measures include:

- Establishing a clear perimeter around your fire.
- Being free from flammable materials.
- Keeping fires manageable.
- Never leave them unattended.

Before leaving your campsite, extinguishing the fire with water and stirring the ashes is necessary.

Adopting these practices can significantly reduce the risks of natural hazards in the wilderness. The key to safely enjoying bushcraft lies in surviving and thriving through a deep understanding and respect for nature's power and unpredictability.

Surviving in Different Climates

Surviving in different climates requires a comprehensive understanding of each environment's unique challenges and hazards. Preparedness and knowledge are your best safety tools, whether in the sweltering heat of a desert, the unpredictable conditions of a rainforest, or the extreme cold of arctic regions.

Hydration is crucial in hot and dry climates as your body loses fluids quickly through sweat, leading to rapid dehydration. Always carry ample water and know how to locate and purify additional sources. Protect your skin and eyes from harmful UV rays by wearing long sleeves, hats, and sunglasses and applying sunscreen. Limit physical exertion during the hottest parts of the day by finding shade or creating a shelter to rest in until temperatures drop. Be aware of heat exhaustion and heatstroke signs, such as headache, dizziness, muscle cramps, and nausea, and take immediate steps for cooling and hydration.

For cold climates, wearing multiple layers helps trap body heat. Focus on materials that retain their insulating properties, like wool or synthetic fibers, even when wet. Staying dry is crucial to avoid hypothermia, so keep your clothing, especially socks, and gloves, dry and be mindful of sweat. Understand the early signs of frostbite, including numbness and pale or hardened skin, and protect extremities with gloves and thick socks. Increase your food intake as your body burns more calories to stay warm in cold environments.

Staying dry is essential in wet and humid climates to avoid hypothermia, even in warm environments. Use waterproof gear and seek shelter during heavy rain. Protect against insects, which are more prevalent and can carry diseases, by using insect repellent and wearing long sleeves and pants. Guard against fungal infections by keeping your skin dry and clean and changing into dry clothes immediately. Always purify water before drinking to avoid waterborne illnesses, as water sources may be abundant but contaminated.

General tips for all climates include familiarizing yourself with basic first aid techniques, such as treating cuts, burns, and bites, and carrying a well-stocked first aid kit. Navigation skills are crucial, so know how to use a compass and map to avoid disorientation. Have the means to signal for help, like a whistle, mirror, or flare; in some situations, a fire can also serve as a signal.

Understanding and respecting the unique challenges of different climates can significantly increase one's chances of surviving and thriving in the wilderness. Preparedness, adaptability, and a calm, informed approach to challenges will serve one well in any environment.

Minimizing Environmental Impact

Understanding how to navigate and endure various weather conditions and environmental hazards is paramount in bushcraft and outdoor survival. However, equally important is our responsibility to minimize our impact on these natural environments. As we venture into the wilderness, it's crucial to adopt practices that preserve the integrity and beauty of these areas for future generations.

One of the fundamental principles of minimizing environmental impact is the concept of Leave No Trace. This approach entails leaving the environment as you found it, or even better, by not leaving any physical evidence of your presence. This can be achieved through several practical measures:

Campsite Selection: Choose a campsite on durable surfaces such as established trails and campsites, rock, gravel, dry grasses, or snow. Avoid altering sites, moving rocks, or vegetation. Camping at least 200 feet from lakes and streams also helps protect riparian areas.

Waste Disposal: Pack out all trash, leftover food, and litter. Utilize catholes (6-8 inches deep) dug at least 200 feet from water sources, camps, and trails for human waste. Cover and disguise the cathole when finished. For washing yourself or your dishes, carry water 200 feet away from streams or lakes and use small amounts of biodegradable soap.

Minimizing Campfire Impacts: Where fires are permitted, use established fire rings, pans, or mound fires. Keep fires small, using only sticks from the ground that can be broken by hand. Burn all wood and coals to ash, put out campfires completely, then scatter cool ashes.

Leave What You Find: Preserve the past by leaving rocks, plants, archaeological artifacts, and other natural objects as you find them. Clean gear and boots before and after your trip to avoid introducing or transporting non-native species.

Wildlife Respect: Observe wildlife from a distance. Do not follow or approach them. Never feed animals, as feeding wildlife damages their health, alters natural behaviors, and exposes them to predators and other dangers.

Minimize Campfire Use: Consider alternatives to fires, such as a lightweight stove for cooking and a lantern for light. Use established fire rings or make a mound fire if you must have a fire.

Be Considerate of Other Visitors: Respect other visitors and protect the quality of their experience. Be courteous. Yield to other users on the trail. Let nature's sounds prevail. Avoid loud voices and noises.

By adhering to these practices, bushcraft enthusiasts ensure their safety and enjoyment and contribute to the conservation of these precious environments. It's a shared responsibility to protect natural habitats, ensuring they remain vibrant and accessible for outdoor adventurers now and in the future. Through mindful actions and a commitment to sustainability, we can all play a part in preserving the wilderness for its intrinsic value and the enjoyment of future generations.

Chapter Summary

- Understanding weather patterns is crucial for safety and preparedness in bushcraft, as it allows one to anticipate and respond to environmental conditions.
- Knowledge of weather systems, cloud formations, wind direction, temperature fluctuations, and barometric pressure is essential for predicting weather changes.
- Natural cues from animals, insects, and plants can also indicate impending weather changes.
- Preparing for extreme weather involves understanding risks, having the right gear,

choosing safe shelter locations, staying hydrated, monitoring health, and planning.
- Avoiding natural hazards in the wilderness includes being cautious around water bodies, navigating through challenging terrain and vegetation, managing encounters with wildlife, and being prepared for weather extremes and fire safety.
- Surviving in different climates requires specific strategies for hydration, sun protection, clothing layers, staying dry, and managing food intake to adapt to hot, cold, wet, and humid conditions.
- It is crucial to minimize environmental impact while engaging in bushcraft and outdoor survival, following Leave No Trace principles to preserve natural environments for future generations.
- Practices for minimizing impact include careful campsite selection, proper waste disposal, minimizing campfire impacts, respecting wildlife, and considering other visitors.

10

ADVANCED FIRST AID TECHNIQUES

Crutches made from sticks in the wilderness.

Suturing Wounds in the Field

In the wilderness, where medical facilities are often miles away, the ability to manage injuries effectively can be life-saving. Suturing is one such skill, particularly for deep or gaping wounds that cannot be closed with bandages alone. This section delves into the essentials of suturing wounds in the field, which requires both knowledge and caution.

Before considering suturing, it's crucial to assess the wound thoroughly. Suturing is appropriate for clean, sharp cuts that are too large to heal correctly. However, puncture wounds, animal bites, or any injuries showing signs of infection should not be sutured closed due to the risk of trapping bacteria inside.

Once you've determined a wound is a candidate for suturing, the next step is ensuring you have the proper tools. A suture kit typically includes sterile needles, thread, scissors, forceps, and antiseptic solution. You might need access to a pre-packaged suture kit in an improvised bushcraft situation. If you must improvise, prioritize sterilization. Needles and thread can be sterilized by boiling them in water or using a flame. However, the latter method requires caution to avoid weakening the material.

Sterilizing the wound and the surrounding skin is equally important. Use an antiseptic solution if available; otherwise, clean, boiled water cooled to a safe temperature can suffice. The goal is to minimize the risk of infection, which can complicate the healing process significantly.

The technique for suturing is delicate and requires practice. Begin by threading the needle and tying a knot at the end of the thread. Use forceps to bring the edges of the wound together gently. Insert the needle through the skin about a quarter-inch from the edge of the wound, ensuring the stitch encompasses both sides of the wound for even closure. The stitches should be spaced about a quarter-inch apart for optimal healing. After completing the suturing, tie off the final stitch securely.

In the days following suturing, it's imperative to monitor the wound closely. Signs of infection, such as increased redness, swelling, warmth, or pus, necessitate immediate attention. If these symptoms arise, the sutures may need to be removed for proper cleaning and drainage.

Finally, understanding when to remove the sutures is as essential as knowing how to place them. Generally, sutures on the face can be removed in about 3-5 days, while those on areas where the skin is under tension, such as the joints, might need to stay in place for up to 10 days. Continually assess the wound's healing progress before deciding to remove sutures.

Suturing is a valuable skill in bushcraft first aid but comes with responsibilities. Proper technique, sterilization, and aftercare are paramount to ensure the best possible outcome for wound healing in the wilderness.

Managing Severe Allergic Reactions

In the wilderness, where medical help may be hours or even days away, it's crucial to understand how to manage severe allergic reactions, also known as anaphylaxis. Anaphylaxis is a rapid, life-threatening allergic response that requires immediate action. This guide will help you identify and manage severe allergic reactions in a bushcraft setting.

Recognizing the signs and symptoms of anaphylaxis is the first step in managing it. These can vary but often include difficulty breathing, swelling of the face, lips, or tongue, hives, abdominal pain, vomiting, diarrhea, a sense of impending doom, and loss of consciousness. The onset can be swift, developing within seconds or minutes of exposure to the allergen, which could be anything from insect stings to food.

Upon recognizing the signs of anaphylaxis, immediate action is necessary. Quickly assess the environment's safety for both the responder and the victim, ensuring no ongoing exposure to the allergen. Send someone to call for emergency medical services immediately. In remote locations, this may involve signaling for help or using a communication device if one is available.

If the individual has a history of severe allergies, they may carry an epinephrine auto-injector (EpiPen).

Administering epinephrine promptly can be life-saving. Familiarize yourself with the instructions for using an auto-injector before you find yourself in an emergency. Remove the auto-injector cap, place the injector against the person's thigh, through clothing if necessary, press firmly until the injector activates, then hold in place for the recommended duration (usually about 10 seconds). Remove the injector and massage the injection site for 10 seconds to enhance absorption.

After administering epinephrine, lay the person flat on their back with their legs elevated to improve blood flow. If breathing is difficult, help them sit up to make breathing easier. If vomiting occurs, turn them on their side to prevent choking. Keep a close eye on the person's breathing and consciousness. If they stop breathing or if their heart stops, be prepared to perform CPR immediately.

Shock can make a person feel cold, so cover them with a blanket or extra layers to help maintain body heat. If symptoms do not improve within 5 to 15 minutes, and you have access to a second epinephrine auto-injector, administer a second dose following the same procedure as the first.

Monitor the person closely once the immediate threat has passed, as anaphylactic reactions can recur, necessitating further treatment. When help arrives, provide a complete account of the incident, including the trigger (if known), the time and dose of epinephrine administered, and any changes in the person's condition.

Prevention is a critical component of managing severe allergic reactions. If you or someone in your group has known allergies, take proactive steps to avoid exposure to known allergens. Carry appropriate medications, including at least two epinephrine auto-injectors, and ensure that everyone in the group knows how to use them.

Understanding and preparing for severe allergic reactions in the wilderness can mean the difference between life and death. You can save a life by recognizing the signs of anaphylaxis, acting quickly to administer first aid, and seeking professional medical help as soon as possible.

Field Management of Dental Emergencies

In the wilderness, where professional dental care is not immediately accessible, managing dental emergencies effectively becomes crucial. This section delves into practical strategies and techniques for addressing common dental issues that may arise in bushcraft scenarios. Understanding these methods can significantly alleviate discomfort and prevent complications until professional help can be sought.

Various factors, including decay, abscess, fracture, or

a lost filling, can cause toothaches. When a toothache occurs, it's essential to rinse the mouth with warm water to clean it and gently use dental floss to remove any food caught between the teeth. If swelling is present, applying a cold compress to the outside of the cheek can offer some relief. It's imperative to avoid placing aspirin or any other painkiller against the gums near the aching tooth, as it may burn the gum tissue. If the pain persists, consider using clove oil (eugenol), which can be applied to the affected tooth or cavity to reduce pain.

If a tooth is broken, chipped, or fractured, rinse the mouth with warm water to clean the area and apply a cold compress to the face to reduce swelling. If the break is minor and there's no pain, it's still important to be cautious about chewing or applying pressure to the affected tooth. For more severe breaks causing pain, temporary dental cement can be applied, if available, to protect the tooth until professional care can be accessed.

A knocked-out tooth presents a dental emergency that requires quick action. One should hold the tooth by the crown (the part usually exposed in the mouth) and rinse off the root of the tooth in water if it's dirty, avoiding scrubbing or removing any attached tissue fragments. Try to reinsert it into the socket gently. If that's not feasible, place the tooth in a small milk container (or water if milk is unavailable) to keep it moist. It's crucial to seek dental assistance as soon as possible since the chances of saving the tooth decrease significantly as time passes.

Sugarless gum can be used as a temporary measure for a lost filling. Chew a piece of gum and then use it to cover the cavity, ensuring it's sugarless to avoid causing pain. For a lost crown, attempt to slip it back over the tooth if it is still intact, coating the inner surface with dental cement, toothpaste, or denture adhesive to help hold the crown in place until professional dental care can be obtained.

An abscess is an infection that occurs around the root of a tooth or in the space between the teeth and gums. Abscesses are severe conditions that can damage tissue and surrounding teeth, with the infection possibly spreading to other parts of the body if left untreated. If an abscess is suspected, seeking professional dental care is vital. In the meantime, rinsing the mouth with a mild saltwater solution several times daily can help draw the pus to the surface and relieve pressure.

While these techniques provide temporary relief and can be crucial in managing dental emergencies in the wilderness, they do not replace the need for professional dental care. It's essential to seek out a dentist as soon as possible to address the underlying issues and receive appropriate treatment. Prevention is always better than cure, so maintaining good oral hygiene practices, even in the wilderness, is critical to avoiding dental emergencies.

Handling Psychological First Aid

In the wilderness, where the unpredictability of nature meets the fragility of the human condition, psychological first aid becomes as crucial as treating physical injuries. This section delves into the nuanced approach required to administer psychological first aid in bushcraft scenarios, emphasizing the importance of recognizing and addressing mental health crises that may arise from high-stress situations.

Psychological first aid in the wilderness begins with establishing safety and security. The first step is ensuring that all individuals involved in a bushcraft expedition are physically safe. Once physical safety is secured, attention must be turned to creating a sense of psychological safety. This involves reassuring individuals, providing accurate information about the situation, and setting realistic expectations for rescue or self-recovery.

Communication plays a pivotal role in psychological first aid. Active listening, without judgment, allows individuals to express their fears, frustrations, and concerns. It's essential to validate these feelings, acknowledging the stress and fear as normal reactions to an abnormal situation. Simple, clear, and calm communication can help reduce anxiety and provide comfort and stability.

Orientation to the present is another critical

component. Individuals experiencing acute stress may become disoriented, confused, or overwhelmed by their thoughts. Gently guiding them to focus on the here and now through mindfulness techniques or simple sensory exercises (such as naming objects they can see, hear, or touch), can help mitigate panic and ground them in reality.

In situations where trauma has occurred, it's crucial to avoid forcing individuals to recount their experiences before they are ready. Instead, offer support and let them know that their reactions are normal and that seeking help is okay. Encourage, but do not pressure, them to share their feelings and experiences at their own pace.

Building community and support among the group can also aid in psychological recovery. Encouraging teamwork, shared responsibilities, and mutual support can foster a sense of belonging and collective resilience. This communal approach can be efficient in bushcraft settings, where reliance on one another is often necessary for survival.

Finally, it's essential to recognize when professional help is needed. Signs that someone may need more than basic psychological first aid include persistent disorientation, severe anxiety or panic attacks, uncontrollable emotions, or thoughts of self-harm. Planning for evacuation or establishing communication with emergency services for psychological support becomes a priority in these cases.

As we transition from addressing immediate psychological needs to considering the longer-term care and planning necessary for recovery, it's clear that psychological first aid is not a one-time intervention but the beginning of a continuous process of support and healing. The skills and principles outlined here are vital for the immediate aftermath of a crisis and the ongoing journey back to normalcy and health.

Evacuation and Long-Term Care Planning

Understanding evacuation principles and long-term care planning is crucial in the wilderness, where professional medical help may be hours or even days away. This knowledge ensures the well-being of the injured and prepares the group for potential challenges during the evacuation process. The aim is to equip you with the necessary skills and knowledge to plan and execute an evacuation effectively and manage long-term care when immediate evacuation isn't possible.

Evacuation planning starts with assessing the injured individual's condition to determine the necessity of evacuation. If the person's life is in danger and cannot be stabilized on-site, evacuation becomes a priority. However, evacuation in the wilderness is complex. It requires careful planning, considering factors such as terrain, weather conditions, the physical condition of the injured, and the distance to the nearest medical facility.

Communication is vital; always carry a means to communicate with emergency services, such as a satellite phone, a personal locator beacon (PLB), or a two-way radio. Before embarking on your journey, inform someone outside your group about your plans and expected return time.

Depending on the terrain and the condition of the injured, evacuation methods can range from manual carries and makeshift stretchers to water transport or even air evacuation if the situation is dire and resources allow.

It's also crucial that at least one group member is proficient in navigation, equipped with detailed maps of the area, a compass, and a GPS device to mark your location and the best route to reach help or guide rescuers to your location.

When evacuation is not immediately possible, providing long-term care becomes essential. This involves creating a stable environment for the injured, monitoring their condition, and administering first aid. Protect the injured from the elements by setting up a shelter and using insulation materials to maintain their body temperature, preventing hypothermia or heatstroke, depending on the weather conditions.

If the injured can eat, keep them hydrated and provide them with energy-dense foods to maintain their strength and aid recovery. Regularly monitor and tend to their injuries, including cleaning wounds, applying fresh bandages, and managing pain while being vigilant for signs of infection or deterioration in their condition.

The mental and emotional state of the injured can significantly impact their physical recovery, so offer constant reassurance, keep them informed about the situation, and engage them in decisions about their care to maintain their spirits.

Keep detailed notes of the injured person's condition, the care provided, and any changes over time, as this information can be invaluable to rescuers or medical professionals when they take over.

In conclusion, being prepared with evacuation and long-term care planning skills is essential, even though the hope is that you'll never need to use them. The wilderness is unpredictable, and knowing how to manage serious injuries can make the difference between life and death. The goal is to stabilize the injured and get them to professional medical care as safely and quickly as possible.

Chapter Summary

- Suturing is a critical skill for managing deep wounds in the wilderness, requiring proper assessment, sterilization, and technique.
- Suturing is suitable for clean, sharp cuts but not for puncture wounds, animal bites, or infected injuries due to the risk of trapping bacteria.
- A suture kit should include sterile needles, thread, scissors, forceps, and antiseptic solution; improvisation requires prioritizing sterilization.
- The suturing process involves threading the needle, using forceps to align wound edges, and spacing stitches for optimal healing. It also involves close monitoring for infection signs.
- Managing severe allergic reactions (anaphylaxis) in the wilderness involves recognizing symptoms, administering epinephrine, and ensuring the victim is warm and monitored.
- Dental emergencies in remote areas can be temporarily managed by rinsing, cold compresses, temporary dental cement, or

reinserting a knocked-out tooth into the socket.
- Psychological first aid focuses on establishing safety, active listening, orientation to the present, and recognizing when professional help is needed.
- Evacuation and long-term care planning in the wilderness require assessing the need for evacuation, communication with emergency services, and providing shelter, hydration, nutrition, and psychological support.

THE JOURNEY AHEAD

A thunderstorm in the wilderness.

Reflecting on What We've Learned

As we pause to reflect on the wealth of knowledge we've amassed throughout our exploration of bushcraft first aid, we must recognize the profound impact this learning can have on our outdoor experiences. The journey from understanding the basics to mastering advanced first aid techniques has equipped us with the skills to respond to emergencies and instilled in us a more profound respect for the natural world and the unpredictability it harbors.

The progression from foundational principles to complex interventions has been deliberate, ensuring that each step builds on the last, reinforcing our competence and confidence. We've learned to assess situations with a critical eye, apply our skills under pressure, and adapt to the challenges presented by remote environments. These are not just lessons in first aid but in resilience, preparation, and the importance of maintaining a calm, focused mindset in the face of adversity.

Our exploration has spanned a broad spectrum of scenarios, from managing minor injuries that can be treated on the spot to addressing life-threatening emergencies that require immediate action and evacuation. We've delved into the intricacies of wound care and fracture management and the critical steps to take in the event of bites, stings, and exposure to the elements. Each topic has been approached with a practical, hands-on perspective, emphasizing the importance of practice and repetition in ingraining these skills into our muscle memory.

However, the acquisition of knowledge is only the beginning. The actual test of our learning lies in its application — not just in emergencies but in our everyday approach to safety, risk assessment, and how we prepare for our adventures. It's about integrating these principles into our planning, ensuring we have the necessary supplies, and making informed decisions about our activities and the environments we choose to explore.

As we move forward, it's crucial to remember that the field of first aid, particularly within the context of bushcraft and wilderness settings, is ever-evolving. New techniques, research findings, and technologies continually shape our understanding of best practices. Staying informed, seeking further education, and practicing our skills regularly are essential steps in ensuring we remain prepared to face whatever challenges the wilderness may present.

In embracing the journey of continuous learning and improvement, we enhance our safety and well-being and contribute to the safety and well-being of those with whom we share our outdoor adventures. The knowledge we carry into the wilderness is a powerful tool that empowers us to face the uncertainties of the natural world with confidence and competence. As we look ahead, let us commit to maintaining our curiosity, seeking new growth opportunities, and upholding the highest standards of safety and preparedness in our bushcraft endeavors.

Continuing Education in Bushcraft First Aid

Now, the importance of continuous learning in bushcraft first aid cannot be overstated. The wilderness is ever-changing, and so are the techniques and knowledge necessary to ensure safety and well-being in these environments. This section aims to guide you in engaging in ongoing education in bushcraft first aid, ensuring that your skills remain sharp and your knowledge up to date.

First and foremost, it's crucial to recognize that learning is a lifelong journey. The completion of a bushcraft first aid course is just the beginning. The real test of your knowledge and skills comes when you're faced with real-life situations that demand quick thinking and decisive action. Commit to regular review sessions of your first aid materials to prepare for these moments. This could mean monthly refreshers on specific techniques or quarterly reviews of your first aid knowledge base. The goal is to keep the information fresh in your mind so you can easily recall it when needed.

Another key aspect of continuing education is staying

abreast of new developments in first aid and wilderness medicine. Medical advice and best practices evolve as new research emerges and techniques are refined. Subscribing to relevant journals, joining professional organizations, and participating in forums dedicated to wilderness first aid are excellent ways to ensure you're always informed about the latest advancements.

Practical experience is also invaluable. Seek opportunities to practice your skills in controlled environments, such as workshops, simulations, and training exercises organized by bushcraft schools or outdoor clubs. These experiences reinforce your existing knowledge and expose you to scenarios you might not have considered before, broadening your understanding and capabilities.

Networking with other bushcraft enthusiasts and first aid practitioners is another beneficial strategy. Sharing experiences and knowledge with peers can reveal insights and tips you might not find in textbooks or formal courses. Moreover, building a network of like-minded individuals creates a support system that you can turn to for advice or assistance when faced with challenging situations.

Finally, consider advancing your education through additional certifications or courses that delve deeper into specific areas of wilderness medicine. Specialized training in trauma care, search and rescue operations, or herbal medicine can significantly enhance your ability to provide adequate first aid in the bushcraft context. These courses expand your skill set and increase your confidence in handling a more comprehensive range of medical emergencies.

In conclusion, the journey of learning in bushcraft first aid is ongoing. By embracing continuous education, staying informed about new developments, gaining practical experience, networking with peers, and pursuing advanced training, you can ensure that you are always prepared to provide competent and effective first aid in the wilderness. Remember, the goal is not just to be ready for emergencies but to prevent them from happening in the first place. Through diligent study and practice, you can achieve this goal and enjoy safer, more rewarding adventures in the great outdoors.

Building a Community of Preparedness

It now becomes increasingly clear that the path to actual preparedness is one we walk with others. The knowledge and skills we acquire, particularly in the realm of first aid, hold the potential to safeguard our own lives and fortify the well-being of those around us. In this spirit, building a preparedness community emerges as a pivotal next step in our collective journey.

The essence of such a community lies in the shared commitment to learning, practicing, and teaching the fundamentals of bushcraft first aid. It's about creating a network of individuals who are equipped to handle emergencies in the wild and passionate about passing on this critical knowledge. This endeavor begins with each of us as we take the initiative to reach out, connect, and engage with fellow enthusiasts through local clubs, online forums, or educational workshops.

Organizing regular meet-ups, whether in person or virtually, can be a powerful platform for exchanging ideas, experiences, and best practices. These gatherings offer invaluable opportunities for hands-on learning, where members can demonstrate first-aid techniques, share insights on navigating medical emergencies in remote settings, and discuss the latest advancements in wilderness medicine. Such interactive sessions reinforce our skills and strengthen the community's bonds, fostering a sense of camaraderie and mutual support.

Moreover, collaboration with local emergency responders and wilderness medicine professionals can elevate the community's knowledge base to new heights. Inviting experts to lead seminars or workshops enriches the learning experience. It bridges the gap between bushcraft enthusiasts and the broader medical community. These partnerships can facilitate access to advanced training, resources, and certifications, further empowering individuals to make a meaningful difference in emergencies.

In fostering a community of preparedness, we also embrace the responsibility of advocacy. Raising awareness about the importance of first aid in wilderness settings, advocating for accessible education, and supporting conservation efforts are all integral to our mission. By championing these causes, we contribute to the safety and well-being of our community and the preservation of the natural environments we cherish.

As we look to the future, let us remember that the strength of our community lies in its diversity, inclusivity, and shared dedication to learning and growth. By coming together, we can create a resilient network of bushcraft practitioners ready to face the challenges of the wilderness with confidence and competence. In doing so, we ensure our own safety and uphold our commitment to the ethical exploration and stewardship of the natural world.

The Ethical Wilderness Explorer

As we journey through the wilderness, embracing bushcraft skills and the essentials of first aid, it becomes imperative to reflect on the broader impact of our adventures. The wilderness is not merely a backdrop for our endeavors but a living, breathing entity that demands respect and ethical consideration. As ethical wilderness explorers, our responsibilities extend beyond personal safety and survival; they encompass a profound respect for the natural environment and a commitment to preserving it for future generations.

The concept of Leave No Trace is foundational to ethical wilderness exploration. This principle guides us to minimize our impact on the natural environment, ensuring that we leave the wilderness as pristine as we found it, if not in better condition. Practicing Leave No Trace involves simple yet impactful actions such as packing out all trash, including biodegradable materials, staying on designated trails to prevent erosion, and setting up campsites at least 200 feet from water sources to protect aquatic ecosystems.

Moreover, ethical wilderness exploration involves understanding and respecting wildlife. This means maintaining a safe distance from animals, not feeding wildlife, and securing food and trash to avoid attracting animals to campsites. Such practices protect the animals and their habitats and ensure the safety of explorers.

Another aspect of being an ethical wilderness explorer is the commitment to sustainable resource use. This includes using renewable resources, such as fallen wood for firewood instead of cutting live trees, and relying on a camp stove when firewood is scarce or when fires are prohibited due to the risk of wildfires. Water sources should be treated with care, using biodegradable soap sparingly and well away from them to prevent contamination.

In bushcraft first aid, ethical wilderness exploration takes on an additional dimension. It involves not only being prepared to address our own emergencies but also being willing to assist others in distress while ensuring that our interventions do not further harm the environment. For instance, when constructing a stretcher from natural materials, choose abundant and renewable materials and ensure that your actions do not unnecessarily damage the surrounding flora.

Finally, being an ethical wilderness explorer means advocating for protecting and preserving natural spaces. This can involve participating in conservation efforts, supporting policies that protect the environment, and educating others about the importance of ethical wilderness exploration.

As we embrace the wilderness with confidence and respect, let us carry the principles of ethical wilderness exploration. By doing so, we ensure that the beauty and majesty of the natural world remain accessible and intact for those who follow in our footsteps. The journey ahead is not just about mastering the skills of bushcraft and first aid; it is about becoming stewards of the wilderness, safeguarding its wonders for the future.

Embracing the Wilderness with Confidence and Respect

We now arrive at a pivotal moment of reflection and anticipation. The wilderness, with its untamed beauty and inherent risks, beckons us to step forward with a blend of confidence and respect. This journey, enriched by the lessons of ethical exploration and the practical skills of first aid, equips us to embrace the wilderness not as conquerors but as humble guests.

Confidence in the wilderness is not born solely from mastering survival techniques or memorizing first aid procedures. It is cultivated through a deep understanding of our environment and physical and mental capabilities. This confidence is a quiet assurance, a readiness to face challenges without underestimating the forces of nature. It is knowing how to respond to a snake bite as much as recognizing when to turn back because the risks outweigh the rewards. Confidence is also in the acceptance that, despite our preparations, the wilderness will always hold the unexpected. It teaches us to be adaptable, to use our knowledge creatively, and to trust in our ability to navigate the unknown.

Respect for the wilderness is the other half of this symbiotic relationship. It acknowledges that we are part of a larger ecosystem, with responsibilities towards its preservation. Respect is shown in our actions, from minimizing our environmental impact to understanding the significance of the flora and fauna we encounter. It recognizes that the wilderness does not bend to our will and that our survival and enjoyment of it depend on our willingness to learn from it and adapt to its conditions. Respect is also in our preparedness to handle emergencies, not just for our sake but to ensure we are not a burden on the natural resources or the local communities that may come to our aid.

The journey ahead in the wilderness, armed with the knowledge of bushcraft first aid, is an invitation to a lifelong learning experience. Each trip is an opportunity to apply what we have learned, make mistakes, grow, and share our experiences with others. It is a chance to strengthen our bond with nature, contribute to preserving these wild spaces, and encourage others to approach the wilderness with the same confidence and respect.

As we close this chapter, let us carry forward the ethos of the ethical wilderness explorer, blending it with the practical skills of bushcraft first aid. Let this knowledge not just be a shield against the adversities of the wild but a bridge that connects us more deeply with the natural world. The journey ahead is not just about surviving the wilderness; it's about thriving within it, learning its secrets, and respecting its power. With each step, let us remember that the most incredible adventures enlighten, challenge, and remind us of our place in the natural order.

Your Feedback Matters

Thank you for joining me on this journey. If the book inspired you, please share your thoughts by leaving a review on Amazon using the QR code below. Your feedback is invaluable and helps guide others. I'm grateful for your time and hope the insights you've gained enrich your quest for knowledge.

ABOUT THE AUTHOR

Alfred Gibson is an author and wilderness survival expert, best known for his Wilderness Mastery Essentials series. With extensive experience in survival training and outdoor education, his work focuses on practical survival hacks and bushcraft first aid. Gibson's expertise has made his books essential for outdoor enthusiasts. Beyond writing, he is deeply involved in exploring and testing survival techniques in the wild.

www.ingramcontent.com/pod-product-compliance
Lightning Source LLC
Chambersburg PA
CBHW051525020426
42333CB00016B/1786